PRENTICE-HALL CONTEMPORARY
PERSPECTIVES IN PHILOSOPHY SERIES

Joel Feinberg and Wesley C. Salmon, *editors*

Alan Ross Anderson	MINDS AND MACHINES
V. C. Chappell	ORDINARY LANGUAGE
Nelson Pike	GOD AND EVIL
George Pitcher	TRUTH
Vincent Tomas	CREATIVITY IN THE ARTS

"I'll be damned. It says, 'Cogito, ergo sum.'"

Drawing by Richter;
© 1958 The New Yorker Magazine, Inc.

MINDS AND MACHINES

Edited by

ALAN ROSS ANDERSON

Yale University

CONTEMPORARY PERSPECTIVES
IN PHILOSOPHY SERIES

PRENTICE-HALL, INC. Englewood Cliffs, New Jersey

Prentice-Hall International, Inc., *London*
Prentice-Hall of Australia, Pty., Ltd., *Sydney*
Prentice-Hall of Canada, Ltd., *Toronto*
Prentice-Hall of India (Private) Ltd., *New Delhi*
Prentice-Hall of Japan, Inc., *Tokyo*

Current printing (last digit):
12   11   10   9   8

Library of Congress Catalog Card Number:
64-11553

Printed in the United States of America
C-58339

CONTEMPORARY PERSPECTIVES

IN PHILOSOPHY

This series is designed to provide a wide group of readers with collections of essays by contemporary philosophers on problems presently under active discussion in philosophical circles. The articles have been carefully selected for their lucidity and intelligibility, revealing the vitality of current philosophy to an audience which would not normally have recourse to professional journals. Each volume consists of articles devoted to a single topic, thereby creating an unusual degree of internal coherence and dialectical unity. In many cases the articles are addressed to one another as replies or rebuttals, or are otherwise built upon earlier essays to carry the discussion forward to new levels of clarity. The editor of each volume contributes an introduction which furnishes the reader with the orientation and general framework for a full understanding of the issues. Although each volume is deliberately restricted in scope, the series as a whole ranges over the entire breadth of philosophy, from aesthetics and philosophy of religion to semantics and philosophy of science.

The series is dedicated to the view that contemporary philosophical perspectives—even on ancient problems—are distinctive, exciting, and fully intelligible to students and other nonprofessionals. The volumes are designed for use as supplementary materials or as components in larger "homemade" anthologies, in both introductory and advanced courses, and for use as basic source materials for student research projects. They enable the teacher to expose students to current philosophy without the usual struggle over library copies of journals. In addition, these anthologies will be useful to scholars in fields bordering on philosophy—for example, law, linguistics, literature, mathematics, physics, psychology, and theology—who wish to find in convenient capsule form the best of recent philosophical thinking on subjects of interest to them. For readers in general, the series provides an opportunity to sample the actual substance and methods of contemporary philosophy.

JOEL FEINBERG
Princeton University

WESLEY C. SALMON
Indiana University

CONTENTS

MINDS AND MACHINES

INTRODUCTION

ALAN ROSS ANDERSON

> There is no security against the ultimate development of mechanical consciousness, in the fact of machines possessing little consciousness now. . . . Even a potato in a dark cellar has a certain low cunning about him which serves him in excellent stead.
>
> Samuel Butler, *Erewhon*

The development of electronic computers in recent years has given a new twist to questions about the relations between "mental" and "mechanical" events, and stimulated an extraordinary amount of discussion. Since 1950 more than 1000 papers have been published on the question as to whether "machines" can "think."

In the face of this fantastic volume of literature, any selection of recent articles for a small anthology such as this must to a certain extent simply reflect the anthologist's tastes (though I offer no apologies for including the late A. M. Turing's article, which has become, within thirteen years, a classic). I do, however, offer apologies to those friends whose recommendations I have failed to follow, and to those who have written worthy articles I have been unable to include. I shall try in a moment to indicate the principles on which the selection of articles was made, but it might help first to consider briefly the philosophical problems involved.

How would we recognize an *entity* (to use a term that does not prejudge the issue as to whether the thing is an organism or a machine) as having a *mind?* We all feel that *people* have minds, and can think; monkeys can also think, in the sense that they can solve some rather simple problems—so can rats, for that matter. Flies and mosquitoes also seem to get along reasonably well, but most of us feel that they don't have minds (in any very serious sense). And whatever we may mean by "having a mind," most of us would probably agree that a cash register has none, nor does even the most sophisticated of existing electronic computers. But just where does the cut-off line come? The following two positions represent the extremes between which most current discussions fall:

(1) We might say that human beings are merely very elaborate bits of clockwork, and that our having "minds" is simply a consequence of the fact that the clockwork is *very* elaborate, or

(2) we might say that *any* machine is merely a product of human ingenuity (in principle nothing more than a shovel), and that though *we* have minds, we can't impart that peculiar feature of ours to anything except our offspring: no machine can acquire this uniquely human characteristic.

Of course we all "know" that human beings have minds, and that computing machines (at the moment) don't; the philosophical problem has in part revolved about what we *mean* when we say such things. Otherwise put: what kind of evidence would compel us to say that a machine had a mind, or could think, or could have feelings? The admission that a machine had such capacities would presumably carry with it a commitment to speak about the machine in the same way that we speak about entities which undoubtedly do have such capacities, i.e., ourselves. ["Don't bother him (it?)—he (it) is thinking." "He (it) is in a bad mood this morning." And so on.]

On the face of it, speaking in such a way of machines has an absurd ring. But there are also other ways of looking at the matter. Admittedly machines cannot at the moment act as well as human beings in some respects, even though there are many things which they do as well or better than people. Computers can play nim, or pennymatching, as well as we can, they can compute faster, and they can fly better. Are there any reasons for believing that it is impossible in principle to construct machines that could also think, feel, have doubts, and so on? And if we were to deny this possibility, how would we be sure that our arguments were rational (rather than exhibiting an unseemly spirit of intolerance or hostility on our part)?

The foregoing may serve at least to give a sample of the kinds of questions which will be considered in the articles to follow. No article deals exclusively with the philosophy of mind, in the traditional sense, and no article will help with technical problems in electrical engineering; the aim here has been rather to emphasize the "and" in "Minds *and* Machines." For this reason I have been forced to exclude many excellent pieces which, while germane to the topic at hand, were written from the point of view of a philosopher with only a tangential interest in machines, or from the point of view of a mathematician or engineer with only a tangential interest in the philosophy of mind. I have listed in the bibliography at the end of this volume a number of articles which may help the reader in pursuing the topic in either direction.

The other principle of selection betrays my conviction that philosophy consists largely of dialectic. The articles have been so chosen as to provide a certain amount of interplay among the contributors—they are, in a sense, talking to each other. Even if one is not interested in taking a stand on the matter, a good bit may be learned about the issues involved from watching (shall I say) a number of good fighters in the ring.

I am grateful to the authors and to editors of the publications in which the essays originally occurred, for their kind permission to reprint these articles. I am also indebted to Keith Gunderson and Wesley Salmon for a large number of helpful suggestions, and to Marvin Minsky for providing me with a copy of his *Steps Toward Artificial Intelligence* (see the bibliography), which was of great value, both from conceptual and bibliographical points of view. And to my wife I am grateful not only for the use of her Mind, but also for her help with a Machine in the preparation of the manuscript.

COMPUTING MACHINERY

AND INTELLIGENCE

A. M. TURING

1. THE IMITATION GAME

I propose to consider the question "Can machines think?" This should begin with definitions of the meaning of the terms "machine" and "think." The definitions might be framed so as to reflect so far as possible the normal use of the words, but this attitude is dangerous. If the meaning of the words "machine" and "think" are to be found by examining how they are commonly used it is difficult to escape the conclusion that the meaning and the answer to the question, "Can machines think?" is to be sought in a statistical survey such as a Gallup poll. But this is absurd. Instead of attempting such a definition I shall replace the question by another, which is closely related to it and is expressed in relatively unambiguous words.

"Computing Machinery and Intelligence," Mind, *Vol. LIX, No. 236, (1950).* *Reprinted by permission of Mrs. Turing and* Mind.

The new form of the problem can be described in terms of a game which we call the "imitation game." It is played with three people, a man (A), a woman (B), and an interrogator (C) who may be of either sex. The interrogator stays in a room apart from the other two. The object of the game for the interrogator is to determine which of the other two is the man and which is the woman. He knows them by labels X and Y, and at the end of the game he says either "X is A and Y is B" or "X is B and Y is A." The interrogator is allowed to put questions to A and B thus:

C: Will X please tell me the length of his or her hair?

Now suppose X is actually A, then A must answer. It is A's object in the game to try to cause C to make the wrong identification. His answer might therefore be

"My hair is shingled, and the longest strands are about nine inches long."

In order that tones of voice may not help the interrogator the answers should be written, or better still, typewritten. The ideal arrangement is to have a teleprinter communicating between the two rooms. Alternatively the question and answers can be repeated by an intermediary. The object of the game for the third player (B) is to help the interrogator. The best strategy for her is probably to give truthful answers. She can add such things as "I am the woman, don't listen to him!" to her answers, but it will avail nothing as the man can make similar remarks.

We now ask the question, "What will happen when a machine takes the part of A in this game?" Will the interrogator decide wrongly as often when the game is played like this as he does when the game is played between a man and a woman? These questions replace our original, "Can machines think?"

2. CRITIQUE OF THE NEW PROBLEM

As well as asking, "What is the answer to this new form of the question," one may ask, "Is this new question a worthy one to investigate?" This latter question we investigate without further ado, thereby cutting short an infinite regress.

The new problem has the advantage of drawing a fairly sharp line between the physical and the intellectual capacities of a man. No engineer or chemist claims to be able to produce a material which is indistinguishable from the human skin. It is possible that at some time this might be done, but even supposing this invention available we should feel there was little point in trying to make a "thinking machine" more human by dressing it up in such artificial flesh. The form in which we have set the problem reflects this fact in the condition which prevents the interrogator from seeing or touching the other competitors, or hearing their voices. Some other advantages of the proposed criterion may be shown up by specimen questions and answers. Thus:

Q: Please write me a sonnet on the subject of the Forth Bridge.

A: Count me out on this one. I never could write poetry.

Q: Add 34957 to 70764.

A: (Pause about 30 seconds and then give as answer) 105621.

Q: Do you play chess?

A: Yes.

Q: I have K at my K1, and no other pieces. You have only K at K6 and R at R1. It is your move. What do you play?

A: (After a pause of 15 seconds) R-R8 mate.

The question and answer method seems to be suitable for introducing almost any one of the fields of human endeavor that we wish to include. We do not wish to penalize the machine for its inability to shine in beauty competitions, nor to penalize a man for losing in a race against an airplane. The conditions of our game make these disabilities irrelevant. The "witnesses" can brag, if they consider it advisable, as much as they please about their charms, strength or heroism, but the interrogator cannot demand practical demonstrations.

The game may perhaps be criticized on the ground that the odds are weighted too heavily against the machine. If the man were to try and pretend to be the machine he would clearly make a very poor showing. He would be given away at once by slowness and inaccuracy in arithmetic. May not machines carry out something which ought to be described as thinking but which is very different from what a man does? This objection is a very strong one, but at least we can say that if, nevertheless, a machine can be constructed to play the imitation game satisfactorily, we need not be troubled by this objection.

It might be urged that when playing the "imitation game" the best strategy for the machine may possibly be something other than imitation of the behavior of a man. This may be, but I think it is unlikely that there is any great effect of this kind. In any case there is no intention to investigate here the theory of the game, and it will be assumed that the best strategy is to try to provide answers that would naturally be given by a man.

3. THE MACHINES CONCERNED IN THE GAME

The question which we put in §1 will not be quite definite until we have specified what we mean by the word "machine." It is natural that we should wish to permit every kind of engineering technique to be used in our machines. We also wish to allow the possibility that an engineer or team of engineers may construct a machine which works, but whose manner of operation cannot be satisfactorily described by its constructors because they have applied a method which is largely experimental. Finally, we wish to exclude from the machines men born in the usual manner. It is difficult to frame the definitions so as to satisfy these three conditions. One might for instance insist that the team of engineers should be all of one sex, but this would not really be satisfactory, for it is probably possible to rear a complete individual from a single cell of the skin (say) of a man. To do so would be a feat of biological technique deserving of the very highest praise, but we would not be inclined to regard it as a case of "constructing a thinking machine." This prompts us to abandon the requirement that every kind of technique should be permitted. We are the more ready to do so in view of the fact that the present interest in "thinking machines" has been aroused by a particular kind of machine, usually called an "electronic computer" or "digital computer." Following this suggestion we only permit digital computers to take part in our game.

This restriction appears at first sight to be a very drastic one. I shall attempt to show that it is not so in reality. To do this necessitates a short account of the nature and properties of these computers.

It may also be said that this identification of machines with digital computers, like our criterion for "thinking," will only be unsatisfactory if (contrary to my belief), it turns out that digital computers are unable to give a good showing in the game.

There are already a number of digital computers in working order, and it may be asked, "Why not try the experiment straight away? It would be easy to satisfy the conditions of the game. A number of interrogators could be used, and statistics compiled to show how often the right identification was given." The short answer is that we are not asking whether all digital computers would do well in the game nor whether the computers at present available would do well, but whether there are imaginable computers which would do well. But this is only the short answer. We shall see this question in a different light later.

4. DIGITAL COMPUTERS

The idea behind digital computers may be explained by saying that these machines are intended to carry out any operations which could be done by a human computer. The human computer is supposed to be following fixed rules; he has no authority to deviate from them in any detail. We may suppose that these rules are supplied in a book, which is altered whenever he is put on to a new job. He has also an unlimited supply of paper on which he does his calculations. He may also do his multiplications and additions on a "desk machine," but this is not important.

If we use the above explanation as a definition we shall be in danger of circularity of argument. We avoid this by giving an outline of the means by which the desired effect is achieved. A digital computer can usually be regarded as consisting of three parts:

(i) Store.
(ii) Executive unit.
(iii) Control.

The store is a store of information, and corresponds to the human computer's paper, whether this is the paper on which he does his calculations or that on which his book of rules is printed. Insofar as the human computer does calculations in his head a part of the store will correspond to his memory.

The executive unit is the part which carries out the various individual operations involved in a calculation. What these individual operations are will vary from machine to machine. Usually fairly lengthy operations can be done such as "Multiply 3540675445 by 7076345687" but in some machines only very simple ones such as "Write down 0" are possible.

We have mentioned that the "book of rules" supplied to the computer is replaced in the machine by a part of the store. It is then called the "table of instructions." It is the duty of the control to see that these instructions are obeyed correctly and in the right order. The control is so constructed that this necessarily happens.

The information in the store is usually broken up into packets of moderately small size. In one machine, for instance, a packet might consist of ten decimal digits. Numbers are assigned to the parts of the store in which the various packets of information are stored, in some systematic manner. A typical instruction might say—

"Add the number stored in position 6809 to that in 4302 and put the result back into the latter storage position."

Needless to say it would not occur in the machine expressed in English. It would more likely be coded in a form such as 6809430217. Here 17 says which of various possible operations is to be performed on the two numbers. In this case the operation is that described above, viz. "Add the number. . . ." It will be noticed that the instruction takes up 10 digits and so forms one packet of information, very conveniently. The control will normally take the instructions to be obeyed in the order of the positions in which they are stored, but occasionally an instruction such as

"Now obey the instruction stored in position 5606, and continue from there"

may be encountered, or again

"If position 4505 contains 0 obey next the instruction stored in 6707, otherwise continue straight on."

Instructions of these latter types are very important because they make it possible for a sequence of operations to be repeated over and over again until some condition is fulfilled, but in doing so to obey, not fresh instructions on each repetition, but the same ones over and over again. To take a domestic analogy. Suppose Mother wants Tommy to call at the cobbler's every morning on his way to school to see if her shoes are done; she can ask him afresh every morning. Alternatively she can stick up a notice once and for all in the hall which he will see when he leaves for school and which tells him to call for the shoes, and also to destroy the notice when he comes back if he has the shoes with him.

The reader must accept it as a fact that digital computers can be constructed, and indeed have been constructed, according to the principles we have described, and that they can in fact mimic the actions of a human computer very closely.

The book of rules which we have described our human computer as using is of course a convenient fiction. Actual human computers really remember what they have got to do. If one wants to make a machine mimic the behavior of the human computer in some complex operation one has to ask him how it is done, and then translate the answer into the form of an instruction table. Constructing instruction tables is usually described as "programing." To "program a machine to carry out the operation A" means to put the appropriate instruction table into the machine so that it will do A.

An interesting variant on the idea of a digital computer is a "digital

computer with a random element." These have instructions involving
the throwing of a die or some equivalent electronic process; one such
instruction might for instance be, "Throw the die and put the resulting
number into store 1000." Sometimes such a machine is described as having
free will (though I would not use this phrase myself). It is not normally possible to determine from observing a machine whether it has a
random element, for a similar effect can be produced by such devices as
making the choices depend on the digits of the decimal for π.

Most actual digital computers have only a finite store. There is no
theoretical difficulty in the idea of a computer with an unlimited store.
Of course only a finite part can have been used at any one time. Likewise only a finite amount can have been constructed, but we can imagine
more and more being added as required. Such computers have special
theoretical interest and will be called infinite capacity computers.

The idea of a digital computer is an old one. Charles Babbage, Luca-
sian Professor of Mathematics at Cambridge from 1828 to 1839,
planned such a machine, called the Analytical Engine, but it was never
completed. Although Babbage had all the essential ideas, his machine
was not at that time such a very attractive prospect. The speed which
would have been available would be definitely faster than a human
computer but something like 100 times slower than the Manchester
machine, itself one of the slower of the modern machines. The storage
was to be purely mechanical, using wheels and cards.

The fact that Babbage's Analytical Engine was to be entirely mechanical will help us to rid ourselves of a superstitution. Importance is
often attached to the fact that modern digital computers are electrical,
and that the nervous system also is electrical. Since Babbage's machine
was not electrical, and since all digital computers are in a sense equivalent, we see that this use of electricity cannot be of theoretical importance. Of course electricity usually comes in where fast signaling is
concerned, so that it is not surprising that we find it in both these con-
nections. In the nervous system chemical phenomena are at least as important as electrical. In certain computers the storage system is mainly
acoustic. The feature of using electricity is thus seen to be only a very
superficial similarity. If we wish to find such similarities we should
look rather for mathematical analogies of function.

5. UNIVERSALITY OF DIGITAL COMPUTERS

The digital computers considered in the last section may be classified
among the "discrete state machines." These are the machines which

move by sudden jumps or clicks from one quite definite state to another. These states are sufficiently different for the possibility of confusion between them to be ignored. Strictly speaking there are no such machines. Everything really moves continuously. But there are many kinds of machines which can profitably be *thought of* as being discrete state machines. For instance in considering the switches for a lighting system it is a convenient fiction that each switch must be definitely on or definitely off. There must be intermediate positions, but for most purposes we can forget about them. As an example of a discrete state machine we might consider a wheel which clicks round through 120° once a second, but may be stopped by a lever which can be operated from outside; in addition a lamp is to light in one of the positions of the wheel. This machine could be described abstractly as follows: The internal state of the machine (which is described by the position of the wheel) may be q_1, q_2 or q_3. There is an input signal i_0 or i_1 (position of lever). The internal state at any moment is determined by the last state and input signal according to the table

		Last State		
		q_1	q_2	q_3
	i_0	q_2	q_3	q_1
Input				
	i_1	q_1	q_2	q_3

The output signals, the only externally visible indication of the internal state (the light) are described by the table

State	q_1	q_2	q_3
Output	o_0	o_0	o_1

This example is typical of discrete state machines. They can be described by such tables provided they have only a finite number of possible states.

It will seem that given the initial state of the machine and the input signals it is always possible to predict all future states. This is reminiscent of Laplace's view that from the complete state of the universe at one moment of time, as described by the positions and velocities of all particles, it should be possible to predict all future states. The prediction which we are considering is, however, rather nearer to practicability than that considered by Laplace. The system of the "universe as a whole" is such that quite small errors in the initial conditions can have an overwhelming effect at a later time. The displacement of a single electron by a billionth of a centimetre at one moment might make the difference between a man being killed by an avalanche a year later, or escaping. It is an essential property of the mechanical systems which we have called "discrete state machines" that this phenomenon does not occur. Even when we consider the actual physical machines instead of the idealized machines, reasonably accurate knowledge of the state at one moment yields reasonably accurate knowledge any number of steps later.

As we have mentioned, digital computers fall within the class of discrete state machines. But the number of states of which such a machine is capable is usually enormously large. For instance, the number for the machine now working at Manchester is about $2^{165,000}$, i.e., about $10^{50,000}$. Compare this with our example of the clicking wheel described above, which had three states. It is not difficult to see why the number of states should be so immense. The computer includes a store corresponding to the paper used by a human computer. It must be possible to write into the store any one of the combinations of symbols which might have been written on the paper. For simplicity suppose that only digits from 0 to 9 are used as symbols. Variations in handwriting are ignored. Suppose the computer is allowed 100 sheets of paper each containing 50 lines each with room for 30 digits. Then the number of states is $10^{100 \times 50 \times 30}$, i.e., $10^{150,000}$. This is about the number of states of three Manchester machines put together. The logarithm to the base two of the number of states is usually called the "storage capacity" of the machine. Thus the Manchester machine has a storage capacity of about 165,000 and the wheel machine of our example about $1 \cdot 6$. If two machines are put together their capacities must be added to obtain the capacity of the resultant machine. This leads to the possibility of statements such as "The Manchester machine contains 64 magnetic tracks each with a capacity of 2560, eight electronic tubes with a capacity of 1280. Miscellaneous storage amounts to about 300 making a total of 174, 380."

Given the table corresponding to a discrete state machine it is possible to predict what it will do. There is no reason why this calculation should not be carried out by means of a digital computer. Provided it could be carried out sufficiently quickly the digital computer could mimic the behavior of any discrete state machine. The imitation game could then be played with the machine in question (as B) and the mimicking digital computer (as A) and the interrogator would be unable to distinguish them. Of course the digital computer must have an adequate storage capacity as well as working sufficiently fast. Moreover, it must be programed afresh for each new machine which it is desired to mimic.

This special property of digital computers, that they can mimic any discrete state machine, is described by saying that they are *universal* machines. The existence of machines with this property has the important consequence that, considerations of speed apart, it is unnecessary to design various new machines to do various computing processes. They can all be done with one digital computer, suitably programed for each case. It will be seen that as a consequence of this all digital computers are in a sense equivalent.

We may now consider again the point raised at the end of §3. It was suggested tentatively that the question, "Can machines think?" should be replaced by "Are there imaginable digital computers which would do well in the imitation game?" If we wish we can make this superficially more general and ask "Are there discrete state machines which would do well?" But in view of the universality property we see that either of these questions is equivalent to this, "Let us fix our attention on one particular digital computer C. Is it true that by modifying this computer to have an adequate storage, suitably increasing its speed of action, and providing it with an appropriate program, C can be made to play satisfactorily the part of A in the imitation game, the part of B being taken by a man?"

6. CONTRARY VIEWS ON THE MAIN QUESTION

We may now consider the ground to have been cleared and we are ready to proceed to the debate on our question, "Can machines think?" and the variant of it quoted at the end of the last section. We cannot altogether abandon the original form of the problem, for opinions will differ as to the appropriateness of the substitution and we must at least listen to what has to be said in this connection.

It will simplify matters for the reader if I explain first my own beliefs in the matter. Consider first the more accurate form of the question. I believe that in about fifty years' time it will be possible to program computers, with a storage capacity of about 10^9, to make them play the imitation game so well that an average interrogator will not have more than 70 per cent chance of making the right identification after five minutes of questioning. The original question, "Can machines think?" I believe to be too meaningless to deserve discussion. Nevertheless I believe that at the end of the century the use of words and general educated opinion will have altered so much that one will be able to speak of machines thinking without expecting to be contradicted. I believe further that no useful purpose is served by concealing these beliefs. The popular view that scientists proceed inexorably from well-established fact to well-established fact, never being influenced by any unproved conjecture, is quite mistaken. Provided it is made clear which are proved facts and which are conjectures, no harm can result. Conjectures are of great importance since they suggest useful lines of research.

I now proceed to consider opinions opposed to my own.

(1) *The Theological Objection.* Thinking is a function of man's immortal soul. God has given an immortal soul to every man and woman, but not to any other animal or to machines. Hence no animal or machine can think.[1]

I am unable to accept any part of this, but will attempt to reply in theological terms. I should find the argument more convincing if animals were classed with men, for there is a greater difference, to my mind, between the typical animate and the inanimate than there is between man and the other animals. The arbitrary character of the orthodox view becomes clearer if we consider how it might appear to a member of some other religious community. How do Christians regard the Moslem view that women have no souls? But let us leave this point aside and return to the main argument. It appears to me that the argument quoted above implies a serious restriction of the omnipotence of the Almighty. It is admitted that there are certain things that He cannot do such as making one equal to two, but should we not believe that He has freedom to confer a soul on an elephant if He sees fit? We might expect that He would only exercise this power in conjunction with a mutation which provided the elephant with an appropriately improved brain to minister to the needs of this soul. An argument of exactly similar form may be made for the case of machines. It may seem different because it is more difficult to "swallow." But this really only means that we think it would be less likely that He would consider the circumstances suitable for conferring a soul. The circumstances in question are discussed in the rest of this paper. In attempting to construct such machines we should not be irreverently usurping His power of creating souls, any more than

---

[1] Possibly this view is heretical. St. Thomas Aquinas [*Summa Theologica,* quoted by Bertrand Russell, *A History of Western Philosophy* (New York: Simon and Schuster, 1945), p. 458] states that God cannot make a man to have no soul. But this may not be a real restriction on His powers, but only a result of the fact that men's souls are immortal, and therefore indestructible.

we are in the procreation of children: rather we are, in either case, instruments of His will providing mansions for the souls that He creates.

However, this is mere speculation. I am not very impressed with theological arguments whatever they may be used to support. Such arguments have often been found unsatisfactory in the past. In the time of Galileo it was argued that the texts, "And the sun stood still . . . and hasted not to go down about a whole day" (Joshua x. 13) and "He laid the foundations of the earth, that it should not move at any time" (Psalm cv. 5) were an adequate refutation of the Copernican theory. With our present knowledge such an argument appears futile. When that knowledge was not available it made a quite different impression.

(2) *The "Heads in the Sand" Objection.* "The consequences of machines thinking would be too dreadful. Let us hope and believe that they cannot do so."

This argument is seldom expressed quite so openly as in the form above. But it affects most of us who think about it at all. We like to believe that Man is in some subtle way superior to the rest of creation. It is best if he can be shown to be *necessarily* superior, for then there is no danger of him losing his commanding position. The popularity of the theological argument is clearly connected with this feeling. It is likely to be quite strong in intellectual people, since they value the power of thinking more highly than others, and are more inclined to base their belief in the superiority of Man on this power.

I do not think that this argument is sufficiently substantial to require refutation. Consolation would be more appropriate: perhaps this should be sought in the transmigration of souls.

(3) *The Mathematical Objection.* There are a number of results of mathematical logic which can be used to show that there are limitations to the powers of discrete state machines. The best known of these results is known as Gödel's theorem, and shows that in any sufficiently powerful logical system statements can be formulated which can neither be proved nor disproved within the system, unless possibly the system itself is inconsistent. There are other, in some respects similar, results due to *Church,*[2] *Kleene, Rosser,* and *Turing.* The latter result is the most convenient to consider, since it refers directly to machines, whereas the others can only be used in a comparatively indirect argument: for instance if Gödel's theorem is to be used we need in addition to have some means of describing logical systems in terms of machines, and

---

[2] Authors' names in italics refer to works cited in the bibliography.

machines in terms of logical systems. The result in question refers to a type of machine which is essentially a digital computer with an infinite capacity. It states that there are certain things that such a machine cannot do. If it is rigged up to give answers to questions as in the imitation game, there will be some questions to which it will either give a wrong answer, or fail to give an answer at all however much time is allowed for a reply. There may, of course, be many such questions, and questions which cannot be answered by one machine may be satisfactorily answered by another. We are of course supposing for the present that the questions are of the kind to which an answer "Yes" or "No" is appropriate, rather than questions such as "What do you think of Picasso?" The questions that we know the machines must fail on are of this type, "Consider the machine specified as follows. . . . Will this machine ever answer 'Yes' to any question?" The dots are to be replaced by a description of some machine in a standard form, which could be something like that used in Sec. 5. When the machine described bears a certain comparatively simple relation to the machine which is under interrogation, it can be shown that the answer is either wrong or not forthcoming. This is the mathematical result: it is argued that it proves a disability of machines to which the human intellect is not subject.

The short answer to this argument is that although it is established that there are limitations to the powers of any particular machine, it has only been stated, without any sort of proof, that no such limitations apply to the human intellect. But I do not think this view can be dismissed quite so lightly. Whenever one of these machines is asked the appropriate critical question, and gives a definite answer, we know that this answer must be wrong, and this gives us a certain feeling of superiority. Is this feeling illusory? It is no doubt quite genuine, but I do not think too much importance should be attached to it. We too often give wrong answers to questions ourselves to be justified in being very pleased at such evidence of fallibility on the part of the machines. Further, our superiority can only be felt on such an occasion in relation to the one machine over which we have scored our petty triumph. There would be no question of triumphing simultaneously over *all* machines. In short, then, there might be men cleverer than any given machine, but then again there might be other machines cleverer again, and so on.

Those who hold to the mathematical argument would, I think, mostly be willing to accept the imitation game as a basis for discussion. Those who believe in the two previous objections would probably not be interested in any criteria.

(4) *The Argument from Consciousness.* This argument is very well expressed in Professor Jefferson's Lister Oration for 1949, from which I quote. "Not until a machine can write a sonnet or compose a concerto because of thoughts and emotions felt, and not by the chance fall of symbols, could we agree that machine equals brain—that is, not only write it but know that it had written it. No mechanism could feel (and not merely artificially signal, an easy contrivance) pleasure at its successes, grief when its valves fuse, be warmed by flattery, be made miserable by its mistakes, be charmed by sex, be angry or depressed when it cannot get what it wants."

This argument appears to be a denial of the validity of our test. According to the most extreme form of this view the only way by which one could be sure that a machine thinks is to *be* the machine and to feel oneself thinking. One could then describe these feelings to the world, but of course no one would be justified in taking any notice. Likewise according to this view the only way to know that a *man* thinks is to be that particular man. It is in fact the solipsist point of view. It may be the most logical view to hold but it makes communication of ideas difficult. A is liable to believe "A thinks but B does not" while B believes "B thinks but A does not." Instead of arguing continually over this point it is usual to have the polite convention that everyone thinks.

I am sure that Professor Jefferson does not wish to adopt the extreme and solipsist point of view. Probably he would be quite willing to accept the imitation game as a test. The game (with the player B omitted) is frequently used in practice under the name of *viva voce* to discover whether someone really understands something or has "learned it parrot fashion." Let us listen in to a part of such a *viva voce:*

Interrogator: In the first line of your sonnet which reads "Shall I compare thee to a summer's day," would not "a spring day" do as well or better?

Witness: It wouldn't scan.

Interrogator: How about "a winter's day." That would scan all right.

Witness: Yes, but nobody wants to be compared to a winter's day.

Interrogator: Would you say Mr. Pickwick reminded you of Christmas?

Witness: In a way.

Interrogator: Yet Christmas is a winter's day, and I do not think Mr. Pickwick would mind the comparison.

Witness: I don't think you're serious. By a winter's day one means a typical winter's day, rather than a special one like Christmas.

And so on. What would Professor Jefferson say if the sonnet-writing machine was able to answer like this in the *viva voce?* I do not know whether he would regard the machine as "merely artificially signaling" these answers, but if the answers were as satisfactory and sustained as in the above passage I do not think he would describe it as "an easy contrivance." This phrase is, I think, intended to cover such devices as the ,inclusion in the machine of a record of someone reading a sonnet, with appropriate switching to turn it on from time to time.

In short then, I think that most of those who support the argument from consciousness could be persuaded to abandon it rather than be forced into the solipsist position. They will then probably be willing to accept our test.

I do not wish to give the impression that I think there is no mystery about consciousness. There is, for instance, something of a paradox connected with any attempt to localize it. But I do not think these mysteries necessarily need to be solved before we can answer the question with which we are concerned in this paper.

(5) *Arguments from Various Disabilities.* These arguments take the form, "I grant you that you can make machines do all the things you have mentioned but you will never be able to make one to do X." Numerous features X are suggested in this connection. I offer a selection:

> Be kind, resourceful, beautiful, friendly (p. 19), have initiative, have a sense of humor, tell right from wrong, make mistakes (p. 19), fall in love, enjoy strawberries and cream (p. 19), make someone fall in love with it, learn from experience (pp. 25f.), use words properly, be the subject of its own thought (p. 20), have as much diversity of behavior as a man, do something really new (p. 20). (Some of these disabilities are given special consideration as indicated by the page numbers.)

No support is usually offered for these statements. I believe they are mostly founded on the principle of scientific induction. A man has seen thousands of machines in his lifetime. From what he sees of them he draws a number of general conclusions. They are ugly, each is designed for a very limited purpose, when required for a minutely different purpose they are useless, the variety of behavior of any one of them is very small, etc., etc. Naturally he concludes that these are necessary properties of machines in general. Many of these limitations are associated with the very small storage capacity of most machines. (I am assuming that the idea of storage capacity is extended in some way to cover machines other than discrete state machines. The exact definition does not matter as no mathematical accuracy is claimed in the present discussion.) A few years ago, when very little had been heard of digital computers, it was possible to elicit much incredulity concerning them, if one mentioned their properties without describing their construction. That was presumably due to a similar application of the principle of scientific induction. These applications of the principle are of course largely unconscious. When a burned child fears the fire and shows that he fears it by avoiding it, I should say that he was applying scientific induction. (I could of course also describe his behavior in many other ways.) The works and customs of mankind do not seem to be very suitable material to which to apply scientific induction. A very large part of space-time must be investigated if reliable results are to be obtained. Otherwise we may (as most English children do) decide that everybody speaks English, and that it is silly to learn French.

There are, however, special remarks to be made about many of the disabilities that have been mentioned. The inability to enjoy strawberries and cream may have struck the reader as frivolous. Possibly a machine might be made to enjoy this delicious dish, but any attempt to make one do so would be idiotic. What is important about this disability is that it contributes to some of the other disabilities, e.g., to the difficulty of the same kind of friendliness occurring between man and machine as between white man and white man, or between black man and black man.

The claim that "machines cannot make mistakes" seems a curious one. One is tempted to retort, "Are they any the worse for that?" But let us adopt a more sympathetic attitude, and try to see what is really meant. I think this criticism can be explained in terms of the imitation game. It is claimed that the interrogator could distinguish the machine from the man simply by setting them a number of problems in arithmetic. The machine would be unmasked because of its deadly accuracy. The reply to this is simple. The machine (programed for playing the game) would not attempt to give the *right* answers to the arithmetic problems. It would deliberately introduce mistakes in a manner calculated to confuse the interrogator. A mechanical fault would probably show itself through an unsuitable decision as to what sort of a mistake to make in the arithmetic. Even this interpretation of the criticism is not sufficiently sympathetic. But we cannot afford the space to go into it much further. It seems to me that this criticism depends on a confusion between two kinds of mistakes. We may call them "errors of functioning" and "errors of conclusion." Errors of functioning are due to some mechanical or electrical fault which causes the machine to behave otherwise than it was designed to do. In philosophical discussions one likes to ignore the possibility of such errors; one is therefore discussing "abstract machines." These abstract machines are mathematical fictions rather than physical objects. By definition they are incapable of errors of functioning. In this sense we can truly say that "machines can never make mistakes." Errors of conclusion can only arise when some meaning is attached to the output signals from the machine. The machine might, for instance, type out mathematical equations, or sentences in English. When a false proposition is typed we say that the machine has committed an error of conclusion. There is clearly no reason at all for saying that a machine cannot make this kind of mistake. It might do nothing but type out repeatedly "$0 = 1$." To take a less perverse example, it might have some method for drawing conclusions by scientific induction. We must expect such a method to lead occasionally to erroneous results.

The claim that a machine cannot be the subject of its own thought can of course only be answered if it can be shown that the machine has *some* thought with *some* subject matter. Nevertheless, "the subject matter of a machine's operations" does seem to mean something, at least to the people who deal with it. If, for instance, the machine was trying to find a solution of the equation $x^2 - 40x - 11 = 0$ one would be tempted to describe this equation as part of the machine's subject matter at that moment. In this sort of sense a machine undoubtedly can be its own subject matter. It may be used to help in making up its own programs, or to predict the effect of alterations in its own structure. By observing the results of its own behavior it can modify its own programs so as to achieve some purpose more effectively. These are possibilities of the near future, rather than Utopian dreams.

The criticism that a machine cannot have much diversity of behavior is just a way of saying that it cannot have much storage capacity. Until fairly recently a storage capacity of even a thousand digits was very rare.

The criticisms that we are considering here are often disguised forms of the argument from consciousness. Usually if one maintains that a machine *can* do one of these things, and describes the kind of method that the machine could use, one will not make much of an impression. It is thought that the method (whatever it may be, for it must be mechanical) is really rather base. Compare the parenthesis in Jefferson's statement quoted above.

(6) *Lady Lovelace's Objection.* Our most detailed information of Babbage's Analytical Engine comes from a memoir by Lady Lovelace. In it she states, "The Analytical Engine has no pretensions to *originate*

anything. It can do *whatever we know how to order it* to perform" (her italics). This statement is quoted by Hartree who adds: "This does not imply that it may not be possible to construct electronic equipment which will 'think for itself,' or in which, in biological terms, one could set up a conditioned reflex, which would serve as a basis for 'learning.' Whether this is possible in principle or not is a stimulating and exciting question, suggested by some of these recent developments. But it did not seem that the machines constructed or projected at the time had this property."

I am in thorough agreement with Hartree over this. It will be noticed that he does not assert that the machines in question had not got the property, but rather that the evidence available to Lady Lovelace did not encourage her to believe that they had it. It is quite possible that the machines in question had in a sense got this property. For suppose that some discrete state machine has the property. The Analytical Engine was a universal digital computer, so that, if its storage capacity and speed were adequate, it could by suitable programing be made to mimic the machine in question. Probably this argument did not occur to the Countess or to Babbage. In any case there was no obligation on them to claim all that could be claimed.

This whole question will be considered again under the heading of learning machines.

A variant of Lady Lovelace's objection states that a machine can "never do anything really new." This may be parried for a moment with the saw, "There is nothing new under the sun." Who can be certain that "original work" that he has done was not simply the growth of the seed planted in him by teaching, or the effect of following well-known general principles. A better variant of the objection says that a machine can never "take us by surprise." This statement is a more direct challenge and can be met directly. Machines take me by surprise with great frequency. This is largely because I do not do sufficient calculation to decide what to expect them to do, or rather because, although I do a calculation, I do it in a hurried, slipshod fashion, taking risks. Perhaps I say to myself, "I suppose the voltage here ought to be the same as there: anyway let's assume it is." Naturally I am often wrong, and the result is a surprise for me, for by the time the experiment is done these assumptions have been forgotten. These admissions lay me open to lectures on the subject of my vicious ways, but do not throw any doubt on my credibility when I testify to the surprises I experience.

I do not expect this reply to silence my critic. He will probably say that such surprises are due to some creative mental act on my part, and reflect no credit on the machine. This leads us back to the argument from consciousness, and far from the idea of surprise. It is a line of argument we must consider closed, but it is perhaps worth remarking that the appreciation of something as surprising requires as much of a "creative mental act" whether the surprising event originates from a man, a book, a machine or anything else.

The view that machines cannot give rise to surprises is due, I believe, to a fallacy to which philosophers and mathematicians are particularly subject. This is the assumption that as soon as a fact is presented to a mind all consequences of that fact spring into the mind simultaneously with it. It is a very useful assumption under many circumstances, but one too easily forgets that it is false. A natural consequence of doing so is that one then assumes that there is no virtue in the mere working out of consequences from data and general principles.

(7) *Argument from Continuity in the Nervous System.* The nervous system is certainly not a discrete state machine. A small error in the information about the size of a nervous impulse impinging on a neuron, may make a large difference to the size of the outgoing impulse. It may be argued that, this being so, one cannot expect to be able to mimic the behavior of the nervous system with a discrete state system.

It is true that a discrete state machine must be different from a continuous machine. But if we adhere to the conditions of the imitation game, the interrogator will not be able to take any advantage of this difference. The situation can be made clearer if we consider some other simpler continuous machine. A differential analyzer will do very well. (A differential analyzer is a certain kind of machine not of the discrete state type used for some kinds of calculation.) Some of these provide their answers in a typed form, and so are suitable for taking part in the game. It would not be possible for a digital computer to predict exactly what answers the differential analyzer would give to a problem, but it would be quite capable of giving the right sort of answer. For instance, if asked to give the value of π (actually about $3 \cdot 1416$) it would be reasonable to choose at random between the values $3 \cdot 12$, $3 \cdot 13$, $3 \cdot 14$, $3 \cdot 15$, $3 \cdot 16$ with the probabilities of $0 \cdot 05$, $0 \cdot 15$, $0 \cdot 55$, $0 \cdot 19$, $0 \cdot 06$ (say). Under these circumstances it would be very difficult for the interrogator to distinguish the differential analyzer from the digital computer.

(8) *The Argument from Informality of Behavior.* It is not possible to produce a set of rules purporting to describe what a man should do in

every conceivable set of circumstances. One might for instance have a rule that one is to stop when one sees a red traffic light, and to go if one sees a green one, but what if by some fault both appear together? One may perhaps decide that it is safest to stop. But some further difficulty may well arise from this decision later. To attempt to provide rules of conduct to cover every eventuality, even those arising from traffic lights, appears to be impossible. With all this I agree.

From this it is argued that we cannot be machines. I shall try to reproduce the argument, but I fear I shall hardly do it justice. It seems to run something like this. "If each man had a definite set of rules of conduct by which he regulated his life he would be no better than a machine. But there are no such rules, so men cannot be machines." The undistributed middle is glaring. I do not think the argument is ever put quite like this, but I believe this is the argument used nevertheless. There may however be a certain confusion between "rules of conduct" and "laws of behavior" to cloud the issue. By "rules of conduct" I mean precepts such as "Stop if you see red lights," on which one can act, and of which one can be conscious. By "laws of behavior" I mean laws of nature as applied to a man's body such as "if you pinch him he will squeak." If we substitute "laws of behavior which regulate his life" for "laws of conduct by which he regulates his life" in the argument quoted the undistributed middle is no longer insuperable. For we believe that it is not only true that being regulated by laws of behavior implies being some sort of machine (though not necessarily a discrete state machine), but that conversely being such a machine implies being regulated by such laws. However, we cannot so easily convince ourselves of the absence of complete laws of behavior as of complete rules of conduct. The only way we know of for finding such laws is scientific observation, and we certainly know of no circumstances under which we could say, "We have searched enough. There are no such laws."

We can demonstrate more forcibly that any such statement would be unjustified. For suppose we could be sure of finding such laws if they existed. Then given a discrete state machine it should certainly be possible to discover by observation sufficient about it to predict its future behavior, and this within a reasonable time, say a thousand years. But this does not seem to be the case. I have set up on the Manchester computer a small program using only 1000 units of storage, whereby the machine supplied with one sixteen figure number replies with another within two seconds. I would defy anyone to learn from these replies sufficient about the program to be able to predict any replies to untried values.

(9) *The Argument from Extra-Sensory Perception.* I assume that the reader is familiar with the idea of extra-sensory perception, and the meaning of the four items of it, viz., telepathy, clairvoyance, precognition and psychokinesis. These disturbing phenomena seem to deny all our usual scientific ideas. How we should like to discredit them! Unfortunately the statistical evidence, at least for telepathy, is overwhelming. It is very difficult to rearrange one's ideas so as to fit these new facts in. Once one has accepted them it does not seem a very big step to believe in ghosts and bogies. The idea that our bodies move simply according to the known laws of physics, together with some others not yet discovered but somewhat similar, would be one of the first to go.

This argument is to my mind quite a strong one. One can say in reply that many scientific theories seem to remain workable in practice, in spite of clashing with E.S.P.; that in fact one can get along very nicely if one forgets about it. This is rather cold comfort, and one fears that thinking is just the kind of phenomenon where E.S.P. may be especially relevant.

A more specific argument based on E.S.P. might run as follows: "Let us play the imitation game, using as witnesses a man who is good as a telepathic receiver, and a digital computer. The interrogator can ask such questions as 'What suit does the card in my right hand belong to?' The man by telepathy or clairvoyance gives the right answer 130 times out of 400 cards. The machine can only guess at random, and perhaps get 104 right, so the interrogator makes the right identification." There is an interesting possibility which opens here. Suppose the digital computer contains a random number generator. Then it will be natural to use this to decide what answer to give. But then the random number generator will be subject to the psychokinetic powers of the interrogator. Perhaps this psychokinesis might cause the machine to guess right more often than would be expected on a probability calculation, so that the interrogator might still be unable to make the right identification. On the other hand, he might be able to guess right without any questioning, by clairvoyance. With E.S.P. anything may happen.

If telepathy is admitted it will be necessary to tighten our test. The situation could be regarded as analogous to that which would occur if the interrogator were talking to himself and one of the competitors was listening with his ear to the wall. To put the competitors into a "telepathy-proof room" would satisfy all requirements.

7. LEARNING MACHINES

The reader will have anticipated that I have no very convincing arguments of a positive nature to support my views. If I had I should not
have taken such pains to point out the fallacies in contrary views. Such
evidence as I have I shall now give.

Let us return for a moment to Lady Lovelace's objection, which stated
that the machine can only do what we tell it to do. One could say that a
man can "inject" an idea into the machine, and that it will respond to a
certain extent and then drop into quiescence, like a piano string struck
by a hammer. Another simile would be an atomic pile of less than critical
size: an injected idea is to correspond to a neutron entering the pile from
without. Each such neutron will cause a certain disturbance which eventually dies away. If, however, the size of the pile is sufficiently increased,
the disturbance caused by such an incoming neutron will very likely go
on and on increasing until the whole pile is destroyed. Is there a corresponding phenomenon for minds, and is there one for machines? There
does seem to be one for the human mind. The majority of them seem to
to "subcritical," i.e., to correspond in this analogy to piles of subcritical
size. An idea presented to such a mind will on an average give rise to
less than one idea in reply. A smallish proportion are supercritical. An
idea presented to such a mind may give rise to a whole "theory" consisting of secondary, tertiary and more remote ideas. Animals' minds
seem to be very definitely subcritical. Adhering to this analogy we ask,
"Can a machine be made to be supercritical?"

The "skin of an onion" analogy is also helpful. In considering the
functions of the mind or the brain we find certain operations which we
can explain in purely mechanical terms. This we say does not correspond
to the real mind: it is a sort of skin which we must strip off if we are to
find the real mind. But then in what remains we find a further skin to be
stripped off, and so on. Proceeding in this way do we ever come to the
"real" mind, or do we eventually come to the skin which has nothing in
it? In the latter case the whole mind is mechanical. (It would not be a
discrete state machine however. We have discussed this.)

These last two paragraphs do not claim to be convincing arguments
They should rather be described as "recitations tending to produce belief."

The only really satisfactory support that can be given for the view expressed at the beginning of Sec. 6, p. 13, will be that provided by waiting for the end of the century and then doing the experiment described. But what can we say in the meantime? What steps should be taken now if the experiment is to be successful?

As I have explained, the problem is mainly one of programing. Advances in engineering will have to be made too, but it seems unlikely that these will not be adequate for the requirements. Estimates of the storage capacity of the brain vary from 10^{10} to 10^{15} binary digits. I incline to the lower values and believe that only a very small fraction is used for the higher types of thinking. Most of it is probably used for the retention of visual impressions. I should be surprised if more than 10^9 was required for satisfactory playing of the imitation game, at any rate against a blind man. (Note: The capacity of the *Encyclopaedia Britannica,* eleventh edition, is 2×10^9.) A storage capacity of 10^7 would be a very practicable possibility even by present techniques. It is probably not necessary to increase the speed of operations of the machines at all. Parts of modern machines which can be regarded as analogues of nerve cells work about a thousand times faster than the latter. This should provide a "margin of safety" which could cover losses of speed arising in many ways. Our problem then is to find out how to program these machines to play the game. At my present rate of working I produce about a thousand digits of program a day, so that about sixty workers, working steadily through the fifty years might accomplish the job, if nothing went into the wastepaper basket. Some more expeditious method seems desirable.

In the process of trying to imitate an adult human mind we are bound to think a good deal about the process which has brought it to the state that it is in. We may notice three components,

(a) The initial state of the mind, say at birth,

(b) The education to which it has been subjected,

(c) Other experience, not to be described as education, to which it has been subjected.

Instead of trying to produce a program to simulate the adult mind, why not rather try to produce one which simulates the child's? If this were then subjected to an appropriate course of education one would obtain the adult brain. Presumably the child-brain is something like a notebook as one buys it from the stationers. Rather little mechanism, and lots of blank sheets. (Mechanism and writing are from our point of view almost synonymous.) Our hope is that there is so little mechanism in the child-brain that something like it can be easily programed. The amount of work in the education we can assume, as a first approximation, to be much the same as for the human child.

We have thus divided our problem into two parts— The child-program and the education process. These two remain very closely connected. We cannot expect to find a good child-machine at the first attempt. One must experiment with teaching one such machine and see how well it learns. One can then try another and see if it is better or worse. There is an obvious connection between this process and evolution, by the identifications

Structure of the child-machine = Hereditary material
Changes "   "   "   " = Mutations
Natural selection = Judgment of the experimenter

One may hope, however, that this process will be more expeditious than evolution. The survival of the fittest is a slow method for measuring advantages. The experimenter, by the exercise of intelligence, should be able to speed it up. Equally important is the fact that he is not restricted to random mutations. If he can trace a cause for some weakness he can probably think of the kind of mutation which will improve it.

It will not be possible to apply exactly the same teaching process to the machine as to a normal child. It will not, for instance, be provided with legs, so that it could not be asked to go out and fill the coal scuttle. Possibly it might not have eyes. But however well these deficiencies might be overcome by clever engineering, one could not send the creature to school without the other children making excessive fun of it. It must be given some tuition. We need not be too concerned about the legs, eyes, etc. The example of Miss Helen Keller shows that education can take place provided that communication in both directions between teacher and pupil can take place by some means or other.

We normally associate punishments and rewards with the teaching process. Some simple child-machines can be constructed or programed on this sort of principle. The machine has to be so constructed that events which shortly preceded the occurrence of a punishment-signal are unlikely to be repeated, whereas a reward-signal increases the probability of repetition of the events which led up to it. These definitions do not presuppose any feelings on the part of the machine. I have done some experiments with one such child-machine, and succeeded in teaching it a few things, but the teaching method was too unorthodox for the experiment to be considered really successful.

The use of punishments and rewards can at best be a part of the teaching process. Roughly speaking, if the teacher has no other means of communicating to the pupil, the amount of information which can reach him does not exceed the total number of rewards and punishments applied. By the time a child has learned to repeat "Casabianca" he would probably feel very sore indeed, if the text could only be discovered by a "Twenty Questions" technique, every "NO" taking the form of a blow. It is necessary therefore to have some other "unemotional" channels of communication. If these are available it is possible to teach a machine by punishments and rewards to obey orders given in some language, e.g., a symbolic language. These orders are to be transmitted through the "unemotional" channels. The use of this language will diminish greatly the number of punishments and rewards required.

Opinions may vary as to the complexity which is suitable in the child-machine. One might try to make it as simple as possible consistently with the general principles. Alternatively one might have a complete system of logical inference "built in." [3] In the latter case the store would be largely occupied with definitions and propositions. The propositions would have various kinds of status, e.g., well-established facts, conjectures, mathematically proved theorems, statements given by an authority, expressions having the logical form of proposition but not belief-value. Certain propositions may be described as "imperatives." The machine should be so constructed that as soon as an imperative is classed as "well-established" the appropriate action automatically takes place. To illustrate this, suppose the teacher says to the machine, "Do your homework now." This may cause "Teacher says 'Do your homework now'" to be included among the well-established facts. Another such fact might be, "Everything that teacher says is true." Combining these may eventually lead to the imperative, "Do your homework now," being included among the well-established facts, and this, by the construction of the machine, will mean that the homework actually gets started, but the effect is very unsatisfactory. The processes of inference used by the machine need not be such as would satisfy the most exacting logicians. There might for instance be no hierarchy of types. But this need not mean that type fallacies will occur, any more than we are bound to fall over unfenced cliffs. Suitable imperatives (expressed *within* the systems, not forming part of the rules *of* the system) such as "Do not use a class unless it is a subclass of one which has been mentioned by teacher" can have a similar effect to "Do not go too near the edge."

The imperatives that can be obeyed by a machine that has no limbs

---

[3] Or rather "programed in" for our child-machine will be programed in a digital computer. But the logical system will not have to be learned.

are bound to be of a rather intellectual character, as in the example (doing homework) given above. Important among such imperatives will be ones which regulate the order in which the rules of the logical system concerned are to be applied. For at each stage when one is using a logical system, there is a very large number of alternative steps, any of which one is permitted to apply, so far as obedience to the rules of the logical system is concerned. These choices make the difference between a brilliant and a footling reasoner, not the difference between a sound and a fallacious one. Propositions leading to imperatives of this kind might be "When Socrates is mentioned, use the syllogism in Barbara" or "If one method has been proved to be quicker than another, do not use the slower method." Some of these may be "given by authority," but others may be produced by the machine itself, e.g., by scientific induction.

The idea of a learning machine may appear paradoxical to some readers. How can the rules of operation of the machine change? They should describe completely how the machine will react whatever its history might be, whatever changes it might undergo. The rules are thus quite time-invariant. This is quite true. The explanation of the paradox is that the rules which get changed in the learning process are of a rather less pretentious kind, claiming only an ephemeral validity. The reader may draw a parallel with the Constitution of the United States.

An important feature of a learning machine is that its teacher will often be very largely ignorant of quite what is going on inside, although he may still be able to some extent to predict his pupil's behavior. This should apply most strongly to the later education of a machine arising from a child-machine of well-tried design (or program). This is in clear contrast with normal procedure when using a machine to do computations: one's object is then to have a clear mental picture of the state of the machine at each moment in the computation. This object can only be achieved with a struggle. The view that "the machine can only do what we know how to order it to do," [4] appears strange in face of this. Most of the programs which we can put into the machine will result in its doing something that we cannot make sense of at all, or which we regard as completely random behavior. Intelligent behavior presumably consists in a departure from the completely disciplined behavior involved in computation, but a rather slight one, which does not give rise to random behavior, or to pointless repetitive loops. Another important result of preparing our machine for its part in the imitation game by a process

---

[4] Compare Lady Lovelace's statement (pp. 20f.), which does not contain the word "only."

of teaching and learning is that "human fallibility" is likely to be omitted in a rather natural way, i.e., without special "coaching." (The reader should reconcile this with the point of view on pp. 18-19) Processes that are learned do not produce a hundred per cent certainty of result; if they did they could not be unlearned.

It is probably wise to include a random element in a learning machine (see p. 10). A random element is rather useful when we are searching for a solution of some problem. Suppose for instance we wanted to find a number between 50 and 200 which was equal to the square of the sum of its digits, we might start at 51 then try 52 and go on until we got a number that worked. Alternatively we might choose numbers at random until we got a good one. This method has the advantage that it is unnecessary to keep track of the values that have been tried, but the disadvantage that one may try the same one twice, but this is not very important if there are several solutions. The systematic method has the disadvantage that there may be an enormous block without any solutions in the region which has to be investigated first. Now the learning process may be regarded as a search for a form of behavior which will satisfy the teacher (or some other criterion). Since there is probably a very large number of satisfactory solutions the random method seems to be better than the systematic. It should be noticed that it is used in the analogous process of evolution. But there the systematic method is not possible. How could one keep track of the different genetical combinations that had been tried, so as to avoid trying them again?

We may hope that machines will eventually compete with men in all purely intellectual fields. But which are the best ones to start with? Even this is a difficult decision. Many people think that a very abstract activity, like the playing of chess, would be best. It can also be maintained that it is best to provide the machine with the best sense organs that money can buy, and then teach it to understand and speak English. This process could follow the normal teaching of a child. Things would be pointed out and named, etc. Again I do not know what the right answer is, but I think both approaches should be tried.

We can only see a short distance ahead, but we can see plenty there that needs to be done.

THE MECHANICAL

CONCEPT OF MIND

MICHAEL SCRIVEN

Is there an essential difference between a man and a machine? To this question many answers have been suggested. One type of answer claims for the man some psychological quality such as intelligence, consciousness, or originality, which is said to be necessarily lacking in the machine. Other examples are introspection, thought, free will, humor, love, correlation of speech and senses. Throughout this paper the sole example of consciousness will be used. The argument follows very similar lines for the other terms. A machine is normally understood to be an artifact, a manufactured mechanical (and possibly electrical) contrivance. It will so be taken here. The purpose of this discussion will be to consider in detail the statement that machines are never conscious.

When it is said that it is impossible for a machine to be conscious, it is not always clear to what extent this is intended to be a logical

"The Mechanical Concept of Mind," Mind, *Vol. LXII, No. 246 (1953). Reprinted by permission of the author and the editor of* Mind.

objection, and to what extent it is empirical. It may be thought that some particular practical obstacle, such as providing a machine with a means of communication, is insurmountable. But it must be remembered that such empirical obstacles may *conceivably* be surmounted: and an argument based on these differences alone is not logically demonstrative. This discussion will not consider *any* such practical differences to be essential differences: thus, the machines to be compared with man will be capable of speech, gesture, perambulation, etc., and sensitive to light, sound, and other environmental conditions. They will be referred to as robots. A robot can do everything that a machine will ever do. The second question then arises: is there any essential difference between robots and human beings?

It may be thought that the original question has been overwhelmed by the considerable assumptions of the last paragraph. In fact this is so only if the question whether a machine can be conscious depends on its successful emulation of the behavior of, say, a man, who, we should all agree, was conscious. For a robot, *ex hypothesi,* is capable of duplicating any human behavior. If a man answers briskly when we whisper his name behind his chair (or criticizes poetry, or declares himself to be in love), we have no doubt that he is conscious. But a machine might respond to the same sound frequencies with the same reply and we should not feel satisfied that it was conscious. The question we seek to answer with our everyday tests is whether a man is conscious or unconscious: whereas of machines we inquire whether they are capable of consciousness or not. We know that the question of consciousness is proper with a man: what concerns us in the case of a machine is not this question, but the question whether this question can sensibly be asked. It is thus not appropriate to demonstrate that a machine is capable of passing tests that would establish its consciousness were it a man, when we have not yet inquired whether a machine is essentially distinct from a man in *nonbehavioral* respects, as far as they are relevant to the question of consciousness. The robot is simply a machine which is indistinguishable from man in behavioral respects. So the important question becomes: "Is a robot essentially distinct from a man?," and the replies to be considered are of the type "Men and not robots are conscious."

Is it blind prejudice which prevents us from extending the franchise of consciousness to robots, when robots can calculate more quickly, react more swiftly, see more clearly, and remember more accurately than men? What is it that they lack when they can do everything? They do what humans do, but they cannot be what humans are: the electric pulse that activates them is not life. Like some spellbound creature of the myths, they have every appearance of life yet they do not live. Years may pass and we are still deceived but if at last one cuts itself and fails to bleed, or in a mindless fury wrecks a building we would start back in horror, exclaiming "A robot! and all the while we thought it lived and breathed." It never felt nor suffered, thought nor dreamed, though never failed to give the signs. We can make machines to plough and harvest, to perform and imitate, but not to feel pleasure or self-pity. These things are possible only to conscious creatures, and no matter how ingenious the mechanism, how complex the behavior of a machine, no matter whether it talks or plays chess, it's no more conscious than a clock. So we feel at first.

The sense of "conscious" in which it is contrasted with "incapable of being conscious" rather than with "unconscious" will be distinguished from the other by the use of a capital letter. In these terms the apparent paradox of sleeping creatures is resolved: for unconsciousness is quite different from Unconsciousness[1]; in fact unconsciousness (and consciousness) entails Consciousness.[1] The question "Is it Conscious?" can be asked of anything. It is absurd to ask of a stone or a stop-watch "Is it conscious?" because it is absurd to talk of it being dead, asleep, drugged or stunned, i.e., unconscious. There are cases where it is very difficult to decide the question of Consciousness. Consider the living things of the world. Ferns and fruit-trees are not Conscious; nor algae, or the insect-eating plants. Protozoa and bacteria are not Conscious. But are jelly-fish Conscious, or earthworms? At what stage does the child in its development from Unconscious germ-plasm become Conscious? Here are cases where living things are not Conscious and cases where we are in doubt. But doubts arise only about living things. Machines are apparently not alive. There are even cases where it is difficult to decide the question of consciousness. For example, a man might have a completely anesthetized cortex, his behavior being controlled by an external operator employing radio waves to operate minute devices inserted at the efferent nerve-ends. Information from the afferent nerves is similarly relayed to the operator. This man is unconscious, a puppet, though outwardly conscious. But such difficulties arise only about Conscious beings.

It may be said that machines approach Consciousness along another path from the living things, that of behavior. They are capable of greater complexity of behavior than the simple creatures we have mentioned. Is complexity of behavior (or degree of organization) essentially

[1]Read as "capital Unconsciousness/Consciousness."

connected with Consciousness: even behavior as complex as a man's? This is our question once again, by now a paler figure than before.

We can sum up the problem very simply. Everyone knows what "conscious" means; everyone knows he is conscious when he is thinking or remembering, watching or reading. But there can be no inner tests of *other* people's mental conditions and we must judge them from without, *if we can judge them at all*. This is where the difficulties begin. First, though it may *in fact* be certain whether a man is conscious or unconscious, we cannot always be certain from watching him or testing his behavior: he may be totally paralyzed and so never move, yet still be conscious; or he may walk and talk under radio control with an anesthetized brain, i.e., while really unconscious. So the outward signs (including speech) are not infallible indications of consciousness. It is therefore quite certain that they are not, even in men, who we know may be conscious, the same thing as consciousness. Second, there is the very different question of deciding whether something is Conscious, i.e., whether it is capable of being conscious. To suggest that evidence of behavior is sufficient to prove the presence of Consciousness is like suggesting that the response of a lift which starts coming up when we press the button proves there is a man inside. In each case the evidence is appropriate *only* if we have the other vital evidence (the inference-license). By itself it is worthless, as far from conclusive as a can-opener is from a meal. Behavior is not attached to Consciousness as thunder is to lightning, nor as a sound to an echo, nor as clouds are to rain, but only as pain is to torture. The one does not guarantee the other but is guaranteed by it. An indefinitely long series of behavioral observations is not equivalent to the observation of consciousness, but there are times when it is wrong to doubt it is a proof, e.g., a man driving a car. A series of behavioral observations is not equivalent to the observation of consciousness and so it is proper to doubt if it *is ever* a proof of Consciousness. There is an essential connection between the capacity for complex behavior and Consciousness; the one is a necessary condition of the other. But it is not a sufficient condition; and though we may decide which living things are Conscious from their behavior, we cannot decide if everything is Conscious from its behavior. Life is itself a necessary condition of Consciousness, and though behavior is a factor which sometimes decides the question whether a certain system is alive, it is again not the only one. The behavior of an antiaircraft gun-predictor system is more complex, organized, and adaptive than that of seaweed, but it is certainly not alive. The seaweed is biochemically, not behaviorally, more complex. Robots, too, are machines; they are composed only of mechanical and electrical parts, and cannot be alive. If it were announced that scientists had discovered a way to create life, they would not be taken seriously if they produced a complex machine as substantiation. It is as if they announced that we can sometimes see objects below the horizon, and proved this on the scientific definition used by astronomers or surveyors, according to which everything below the horizontal line of sight is below the horizon, e.g., the ground at one's feet. The fact that there may occur in machines as in living organisms the same feature of directive organic unity is not enough to show that both live. It is scarcely surprising that we can produce a mechanism which has this comparatively simple property. It would be extremely surprising if the production of such a mechanism was supposed to endow it with life. There are other tests which are relevant, and these it fails, simple though they are. Since it is nonsense to talk of a machine being dead, it it nonsense to talk of it being alive. Machines do not even belong to the *category* of things which can be dead or alive. It would, of course, be possible to employ organic materials in constructing the robot, but this would not alter the argument. Even if it proved possible to create living cells and incorporate these, the result would not be a conscious machine, because a sufficient proportion to justify calling the thing itself (rather than parts of it) alive and hence possibly conscious would certainly be enough to prevent it being correctly called a machine. This is the last expedient and, like its predecessors, affords no escape from the conclusion that there can be no such thing as a conscious machine.

SUMMARY

There appears to be a paradox associated with the concept of a conscious machine. On the one hand it does not seem that there is anything in the construction, constituents, or behavior of the human being which it is essentially impossible for science to duplicate and synthesize. On the other hand there seem to be some important and meaningful descriptions of human behavior which can never be properly applied to machines. We feel puzzled that the basis for a description can be reproduced, yet the description cannot be reapplied.

This conflict once led people to deny the material composition of the body: in more recent times it has led people to deny that men have any attributes which must forever evade machines.

But only puzzles and problems have solutions: paradoxes have none, only sometimes resolutions. When we resolve a paradox, we do not decide in favor of one of the conflicting arguments and against the other; rather, we bring out the precise truth of each in order to show they do not conflict on the same ground. This is true of the familiar logical and pragmatic paradoxes as well as of those paradoxes at the root of philosophical problems such as the one considered in this discussion. Here we have come to see that the human being need have no transscendent element, yet that machines will never be conscious, because we have come to see that a reproduction of a man sufficiently exact to be conscious is too exact to be still a machine.

APPLICATIONS

It is necessary to discuss separately the application of analytical results such as those evolved here. The question to be decided is whether every possible machine is essentially distinct from a man. One particular answer considered suggests that a machine will never be conscious. The key words are "machine" and "conscious." Now it is entirely possible that the meaning of these words may change, hence that statements involving them may no longer stand in the same logical relation to other statements as they do now. This may occur for a variety of reasons: the most likely is that the forceful associations produced by them will lead to their employment in places where their strict meanings and less forceful associations render it inappropriate or incorrect. An example of this arises in connection with the word "intelligent." One can well imagine a man whose work lies largely with one of the great electronic computers coming to apply this word to it. He often makes mistakes: it is faultless. His memory for figures is limited: it has an enormous storage capacity. He is intelligent, yet the machine is better at the job. At first as slang, then seriously, these machines will be called intelligent. A means for comparing the intelligence of different machines will perhaps be devised: connected with their speed and accuracy of working rather than mere capacity; perhaps also with their versatility and ease of programing. As better computers are produced, and they come to be used less for performing particular calculations than for solving complete problems, the notion of *consulting* a computer, rather than *using* one, will grow. In various other ways usage will reflect the increasing tendency to regard a computer as a specialist *par excellence*. Then one day a man may ask: "Can machines ever be really intelligent?"

This is not one of the questions we have considered, though the words are the same. We have not given an answer for it, nor an indication of one: it is feasible to consider all possible machines, absurd to consider all possible meanings of the word "machine," or "intelligence."

Yet there are circumstances in which it is difficult to decide whether the descriptions employed or the statements made exhibit a change of meaning in their terms, or merely an unprecedented but not improper combination of terms. An example of an unprecedented combination which would involve no change of meaning is the description "blue grapefruit." An example of a change of meaning has just been discussed: it was suggested that the word "intelligent" had changed its meaning when it came to be applied to a computer. In the present meaning of the word it is not sensible to talk of a slide rule or an abacus as intelligent, and the fact that they may be driven by a motor instead of being moved by our hands does nothing towards making them intelligent. An electronic computer is a complicated instrument which we operate for the same purpose as the slide rule and abacus. Unless operated by an intelligent being it is entirely useless: but even when it is operated by an intelligent being, it does not thereby become intelligent, only useful. It may be entirely similar in construction to a human brain; but the human brain is a physiological mechanism, no more intelligent than a muscle. Certainly the brain is an indispensable component of an intelligent being, unlike a muscle, and the relative intelligence of various creatures may be deducible from their brain structure. But it is the creature that is intelligent, not the brain: people have good brains or mediocre brains, but never intelligent brains: it is they who are intelligent. Now computers are not even as well placed in this competition as brains; for they are not indispensable to anyone's intelligence, any more than books are indispensable to memory. And one can no more say that a computer is intelligent than that a book remembers. This is the argument that shows "intelligent" to be an improper adjective for the noun "computer." It is also the argument that shows there has been a change of meaning in one of these terms if the combination has a proper use. In the situation described above, there is a proper, though perhaps only a technical, use for this description. So there has been a change of meaning. Similarly, to consider a very simple example, we can say quite definitely that if there is ever a standard use of the description "childless parent," then the meaning of one of these terms has changed.

Now it was argued in the first part of this paper that the description "conscious machine" could have no proper use. In normal usage, it was suggested, the factors which contribute to the identification of machines are also factors which distinguish them from animate matter and a fortiori from conscious beings. Conversely, the factors which lead us to use the adjective "conscious" include, explicitly or tacitly, the condition that the subject of description is not a mechanical contrivance. Should we be misled on this point, the subsequent discovery of inorganic composition and electric motivation would make us withdraw the adjective, in exactly the way we should withdraw the adjective "angry" from the description of an action by a man whom we later discover to have been acting. There is no difference between the behavior of the robot and a conscious man, between that of the actor and an angry man. But the robot is not in fact conscious, just as the actor is not in fact angry. It follows from this that if we do use the description "conscious machine," one of these terms must have changed in meaning.

But there is a converse situation, in which we are not at first suffering from inadequate information, but instead we are suddenly faced with the crime accomplished, the impossibility completed. Explorers land on another planet and on their return are accompanied by one of the inhabitants, a robot. He is a member of an extensive and cultured civilization, a skilled and learned citizen, anthropoid in appearance, yet with some unusual powers. He spends many months on Earth, observing our social and economic structures with interest. It must be expected that in such circumstances many of the people that get to know him would talk of him in human terms. Suppose that someone suggested that this robot was an example of a conscious machine. It is not as simple to point out a fundamental incongruity in this description as it would be in any proposed application of the description "childless parent," or even of the description "intelligent computer."

But consider now how we should answer the persistent skeptic who refuses to believe that the robot is really a conscious machine. We might point out that the robot has been with us for some time and that we have got to know him as a friend and as a learned colleague. We would ask how this could be possible unless the robot was a conscious being, one genuinely capable of sympathy, of thought, and of inner reflection. There is here no possibility that the skeptic can repeat the technique used to bring out the impossibility of an intelligent computer, for the robot is an autonomous creature, in no normal sense a mere instrument: and some autonomous beings can properly be called "conscious."

The skeptic first asks, Is it properly called a machine? True, he says, it is metallic and mechanical in appearance, both external and internal.

Perhaps it is this alone that marks a machine, he says. But surely it is not enough for it to have this appearance. We must be certain that at every stage the behavior of the components, and in large, of the robot itself is mechanical. For else it may be that the real origin of its movements, speech, and gestures is some nonmechanical influence—a soul perhaps, or an alien being. Moreover, he says, it will not even then suffice to understand the general nature of each connection: to be certain that this robot is only a machine we must make sure that each part is quantitatively mechanical, that the measure of each response is exactly deducible from the measure of each stimulus together with the nature of the linkages. We must in fact, be able to see clearly that this is nothing more than a machine, that it has no "will" of its own. Had we constructed it ourselves, of course, most people would have felt satisfied on this point. Suppose that we are successful in this analysis of the mechanism. Then it might be the case that we could easily predict every move of the robot. More probably, as with the big computers, although it would be possible in *principle* to predict every move, it would rarely be possible to do this as quickly as the machine acts. There is a sense in which one might say that the behavior of human beings is in principle predictable, meaning that one believes them to be no exception to the materialist conception of nature, while not suggesting that on present knowledge we can predict their behavior. In a slightly different sense one might say that the behavior of a roulette wheel or the failure of an engine which suddenly breaks down is in principle predictable. When it is said here that we cannot be certain that the robot is a machine until we are certain that its behavior is in principle predictable, however, it would follow that given time one could calculate the behavior resulting from any given environmental stimuli. It does not follow that we can always say what the robot will do in a certain situation before he does it.

Now the relation between Consciousness and free will is a rather complicated one. It is not easy to prove that the one is impossible without the other. But it is at least certain that we cannot prove that the robot is Conscious. For we now have a complete causal explanation of all its behavior, and this explanation does not at any stage depend on its consciousness, and so its behavior cannot be a proof of the possession of consciousness. Consciousness is not a property which can be detected in a machine by any physical examination, because it cannot be *identified* with any physical characteristics of a machine. Nor can it even be correlated with them, as the color red can be correlated with certain wavelengths of light. The fundamental element in these correlations is the subjective impression and it is exactly this element whose presence in the robot is in question. For example, if we noticed increases in the robot's alpha rhythm which nearly always correlated with the beginning of activity or speech, we might be tempted to say that this was the mark of consciousness. Equally well, however, it might be called a mark of mechanical preparation for speech or activity.

It is only philosophers who have doubted whether we can prove other people are conscious. They tend to do this partly because of the sources of error attendant on a diagnosis of certain mental states from other people's behavior, which are absent from one's knowledge of these mental states in oneself. This is a philosophical and not a scientific doubt because there is (and could be) no correlation of the suggested difference with any scientifically observable differences. The doubt whether a robot can be conscious is not only philosophical but scientific because there are physical (not behavioral) differences between man and robot.

The case is in fact rather stronger than this, as the skeptic would point out. For there is a peculiar weakness about the claim that a robot may be conscious although its behavior is entirely determined (whether or not it has free will). Suppose the robot suggests that the question of its consciousness is surely best known to itself, gives a good explanation of what the word means, and then claims to be conscious. Since we have exact knowledge of its mechanism, one might think that one could then determine whether it was lying and so finally decide the question of its consciousness. But to decide whether it is lying or not when it claims to be conscious one must first decide whether it is conscious or not, i.e., answer the original question. To decide if human beings are lying without knowing the truth ourselves we can use a lie-detector, but these depend on the effects of consciously uttering a falsehood and any comparable test on the robot would be impossible unless it could be decided whether it was ever conscious. A gramophone may produce lies but it does not lie; nor does it tell the truth. So the robot's testimony is of no value, because we cannot show that it is its own testimony. A robot, unlike a gramophone, has its own voice; but what it can say depends on how it is made and for what purpose. Again, we are troubled by doubts whether it is proper to speak of a machine when we cannot say whether or for what it was designed, whether it has ancestors and descendents or designers and mechanics.

In the first part of this paper, we worked on the basis of a fairly simple idea (an unanalyzed concept) of machine and living organism. In this part, we have considered the case of a discovered robot with an unspecified background in an attempt to derive the minimum conditions for calling it a machine and Conscious. Having decided it is a machine on the minimum grounds, we find it still seems possible to *say* the robot is Conscious. But Consciousness has then become something entirely apart from the behavior, a spectral Observer whose presence is without trace or influence. It is not true to say that consciousness is *necessary* to explain certain behavior in machines (e.g., the use of certain language); although one may feel that consciousness *goes with* certain behavior by machines, it does not *follow from* it, as it does with men. Machines that seem to use the word "conscious" correctly, do so simply because they are programed in a certain way: if there was any other explanation, they would not be merely machines.

The background of neglected characteristics here becomes important. If we find the robots on their native planet growing up like children, learning to think and speak, in some way becoming parents and dying, we might be convinced that the usual categories of "machine" and "living organism" need supplementation with a third, perhaps "android." It would then display a lack of understanding of the geography of the new concepts to ask if androids were really machines, but we might call them Conscious. If, instead, they emerge full-grown from automatic factories, the products of one factory being identical in general appearance, in their unchanging facial expression, their abilities and their vocabularies, we should perhaps judge them sufficiently well described as "machines." Perhaps, too, we might even here want to say they were Conscious, for men often tend to personify the machines with which they are familiar: but this would not constitute a good reason for believing they are really Conscious. If we did not have a causal explanation of their behavior, if there were no valves and wheels inside them but only homogeneous plastic, or a cavity, the ascription of Consciousness could be readily understood as that age-old resource of ignorance, the anthropomorphizing move. As it is, their behavior is evidence of their construction, not their Consciousness. Now, it is true that our understanding of the robot mechanism does not make its behavior more predictable, or less human (for we have assumed it behaves as a human): and so we are tempted to explain away the surprise and the humanity by saying it must be Conscious, as a human. Yet, though clocks are predictable, barographs and computers are not; and no one suggests they are Conscious. It is not the unpredictability but the apparent humanity of the robots that produces the reaction of saying they are Conscious. But they appear human simply because they were made to appear human. If there is some reason for doubting whether they were designed and made at all, as in the case of the androids, we count them Conscious but not machines. If there is no such reason, we count them machines, but to count them Conscious is to put the ghost of a ghost in the machine.

Addendum (1963)

This paper can be taken as a statement of the difficulties in (and was written partly as a reaction to) Turing's extention of behaviorism into the computer field [see the preceding article]. Since writing it, I have come to see that there are ways of handling many of these difficulties. For example, one can have overwhelming inductive support for the veracity of an agent (artificial or otherwise) from areas not involving his introspective reports and extrapolate it to support a report of consciousness of pain, provided great care is taken in teaching the language of feelings. [See "The Compleat Robot: A Preface to Androidology," cited in the bibliography at the end of this volume.] And it now seems possible to say what facilities a computer-based system must have in order to make it capable of true comprehension of language. [See *Computers & Comprehension*, RAND publication, forthcoming (with M. Kochen, *et al.*).] I now believe that it is possible so to construct a supercomputer as to make it wholly unreasonable to deny that it had feelings.

MINDS,

MACHINES AND

GÖDEL

J. R. LUCAS

Gödel's theorem seems to me to prove that Mechanism is false, that is, that minds cannot be explained as machines. So also has it seemed to many other people: almost every mathematical logician I have put the matter to has confessed to similar thoughts, but has felt reluctant to commit himself definitely until he could see the whole argument set out, with all objections fully stated and properly met.[1] This I attempt to do.

Gödel's theorem states that in any consistent system which is strong enough to produce simple arithmetic there are formulae which cannot

---

"Minds, Machines and Gödel," Philosophy, *Vol. XXXVI (1961). Reprinted by permission of the author and the editor of* Philosophy.

[1] See A. M. Turing, "Computing Machinery and Intelligence" (above), K. R. Popper, "Indeterminism in Quantum Physics and Classical Physics," Paul Rosenbloom, *Elements of Mathematical Logic,* pp. 207f. Ernest Nagel and James R. Newman, *Gödel's Proof,* pp. 100ff, and Hartley Rogers, *Theory of Recursive Functions and Effective Computability,* pp. 152ff. (all listed in the bibliography at the end of this volume).

be proved-in-the-system, but which we can see to be true. Essentially, we consider the formula which says, in effect, "This formula is unprovable-in-the-system." If this formula were provable-in-the-system, we should have a contradiction: for if it were provable-in-the-system, then it would not be unprovable-in-the-system, so that "This formula is un-provable-in-the-system" would be false: equally, if it were provable-in-the-system, then it would not be false, but would be true, since in any consistent system nothing false can be proved-in-the-system, but only truths. So the formula "This formula is unprovable-in-the-system" is not provable-in-the-system, but unprovable-in-the-system. Further, if the formula "This formula is unprovable-in-the-system" is unprovable-in-the-system, then it is true that that formula is unprovable-in-the-system, that is, "This formula is unprovable-in-the-system" is true.

The foregoing argument is very fiddling, and difficult to grasp fully: it is helpful to put the argument the other way round, consider the possibility that "This formula is unprovable-in-the-system" might be false, show that that is impossible, and thus that the formula is true; whence it follows that it is unprovable. Even so, the argument remains persistently unconvincing: we feel that there must be a catch in it some-where. The whole labor of Gödel's theorem is to show that there is no catch anywhere, and that the result can be established by the most rigorous deduction; it holds for all formal systems which are (i) con-sistent, (ii) adequate for simple arithmetic—i.e., contain the natural numbers and the operations of addition and multiplication—and it shows that they are incompete—i.e., contain unprovable, though perfectly meaningful, formulae, some of which, moreover, we, standing outside the system, can see to be true.

Gödel's theorem must apply to cybernetical machines, because it is of the essence of being a machine, that it should be a concrete instantia-tion of a formal system. It follows that given any machine which is consistent and capable of doing simple arithmetic, there is a formula which it is incapable of producing as being true—i.e., the formula is unprovable-in-the-system—but which we can see to be true. It follows that no machine can be a complete or adequate model of the mind, that minds are essentially different from machines.

We understand by a cybernetical machine an apparatus which per-forms a set of operations according to a definite set of rules. Normally we "program" a machine: that is, we give it a set of instructions about what it is to do in each eventuality; and we feed in the initial "infor-mation" on which the machine is to perform its calculations. When we consider the possibility that the mind might be a cybernetical mechanism we have such a model in view; we suppose that the brain is composed of complicated neural circuits, and that the information fed in by the senses is "processed" and acted upon or stored for future use. If it is such a mechanism, then given the way in which it is programed—the way in which it is "wired up"—and the information which has been fed into it, the response—the "output"—is determined, and could, granted sufficient time, be calculated. Our idea of a machine is just this, that its behavior is completely determined by the way it is made and the incoming "stimuli": there is no possibility of its acting on its own: given a certain form of construction and a certain input of information, then it must act in a certain specific way. We, however, shall be concerned not with what a machine *must* do, but with what it *can* do. That is, instead of considering the whole set of rules which together determine exactly what a machine will do in given circumstances, we shall consider only an outline of those rules, which will delimit the possible responses of the machine, but not completely. The complete rules will determine the operations completely at every stage; at every stage there will be a definite instruction, e.g., "If the number is prime and greater than two add one and divide by two: if it is not prime, divide by its smallest factor": we, however, will consider the possibility of there being alternative instructions, e.g., "In a fraction you may divide top and bottom by *any* number which is a factor of both numerator and denominator." In thus relaxing the specification of our model, so that it is no longer completely determinist, though still entirely mechanistic, we shall be able to take into account a feature often proposed for mechanical models of the mind, namely that they should contain a randomizing device. One could build a machine where the choice between a number of alternatives was settled by, say, the number of radium atoms to have disintegrated in a given container in the past-half-minute. It is *prima facie* plausible that our brains should be liable to random effects: a cosmic ray might well be enough to trigger off a neural impulse. But clearly in a machine a randomizing device could not be introduced to choose any alternative whatsoever: it can only be permitted to choose between a number of allowable alternatives. It is all right to add *any* number chosen at random to both sides of an equation, but not to add one number to one side and another to the other. It is all right to choose to prove one theorem of Euclid rather than another, or to use one method rather than another, but not to "prove" something which is not true, or to use a "method of proof" which is not valid. Any randomizing devices must allow choices only between those operations which will not lead to inconsistency: which is exactly what the relaxed specification of our model specifies. Indeed, one might put it this way: Instead of considering what a completely determined machine *must* do, we shall consider what a machine might be able to do if it had a randomizing device that acted whenever there were two or more operations possible, none of which could lead to inconsistency.

If such a machine were built to produce theorems about arithmetic (in many ways the simplest part of mathematics), it would have only a finite number of components, and so there would be only a finite number of types of operation it could do, and only a finite number of initial assumptions it could operate on. Indeed, we can go further, and say that there would only be a *definite* number of types of operation, and of initial assumptions, that could be built into it. Machines are definite: anything which was indefinite or infinite we should not count as a machine. Note that we say number of *types* of operation, not number of operations. Given sufficient time, and provided that it did not wear out, a machine could go on repeating an operation indefinitely: it is merely that there can be only a definite number of different *sorts* of operation it can perform.

If there are only a definite number of types of operation and initial assumptions built into the system, we can represent them all by suitable symbols written down on paper. We can parallel the operation by rules ("rules of inference" or "axiom schemata") allowing us to go from one or more formulae (or even from no formula at all) to another formula, and we can parallel the initial assumptions (if any) by a set of initial formulae ("primitive propositions," "postulates" or "axioms"). Once we have represented these on paper, we can represent every single operation: all we need do is to give formulae representing the situation before and after the operation, and note which rule is being invoked. We can thus represent on paper any possible sequence of operations the machine might perform. However long the machine went on operating, we could, given enough time, paper and patience, write down an analogue of the machine's operations. This analogue would in fact be a formal proof: every operation of the machine is represented by the application of one of the rules: and the conditions which determine for the machine whether an operation can be performed in a certain situation become, in our representation, conditions which settle whether a rule can be applied to a certain formula, i.e., formal conditions of applicability. Thus, construing our rules as rules of inference, we shall have a proof-sequence of for-

mulae, each one being written down in virtue of some formal rule of
inference having been applied to some previous formula or formulae
(except, of course, for the initial formulae, which are given because they
represent initial assumptions built into the system). The conclusions
it is possible for the machine to produce as being true will therefore
correspond to the theorems that can be proved in the corresponding
formal system. We now construct a Gödelian formula in this formal
system. This formula cannot be *proved-in-the-system*. Therefore the
machine cannot produce the corresponding formula as being true. But
we can see that the Gödelian formula is true: any rational being could
follow Gödel's argument, and convince himself that the Gödelian formula, although unprovable-in-the-given-system, was nonetheless—in fact,
for that very reason—true. Now any mechanical model of the mind
must include a mechanism which can enunciate truths of arithmetic,
because this is something which minds can do: in fact, it is easy to produce mechanical models which will in many respects produce truths of
arithmetic far better than human beings can. But in this one respect
they cannot do so well: in that for every machine there is a truth which
it cannot produce as being true, but which a mind can. This shows that
a machine cannot be a complete and adequate model of the mind. It
cannot do *everything* that a mind can do, since however much it can do,
there is always something which it cannot do, and a mind can. This is
not to say that we cannot build a machine to simulate *any* desired piece
of mind-like behavior: it is only that we cannot build a machine to
simulate *every* piece of mind-like behavior. We can (or shall be able to
one day) build machines capable of reproducing bits of mind-like behavior, and indeed of outdoing the performances of human minds: but
however good the machine is, and however much better it can do in
nearly all respects than a human mind can, it always has this one weakness, this one thing which it cannot do, whereas a mind can. The
Gödelian formula is the Achilles' heel of the cybernetical machine. And
therefore we cannot hope ever to produce a machine that will be able
to do all that a mind can do: we can never, not even in principle, have
a mechanical model of the mind.

This conclusion will be highly suspect to some people. They will
object first that we cannot have it both that a machine *can* simulate *any*
piece of mind-like behavior and that it *cannot* simulate *every* piece. To
some it is a contradiction: to them it is enough to point out that there is
no contradiction between the fact that for any natural number there
can be produced a greater number and the fact that a number cannot

be produced greater than every number. We can use the same analogy also against those who, finding a formula their first machine cannot produce as being true, concede that that machine is indeed inadequate, but thereupon seek to construct a second, more adequate, machine, in which the formula *can* be produced as being true. This they can indeed do: but then the second machine will have a Gödelian formula all of its own, constructed by applying Gödel's procedure to the formal system which represents its (the second machine's) own enlarged scheme of operations. And this formula the second machine will not be able to produce as being true, while a mind will be able to see that it is true. And if now a third machine is constructed, able to do what the second machine was unable to do, exactly the same will happen: there will be yet a third formula, the Gödelian formula for the formal system corresponding to the third machine's scheme of operations, which the third machine is unable to produce as being true, while a mind will still be able to see that it is true. And so it will go on. However complicated a machine we construct, it will, if it is a machine, correspond to a formal system, which in turn will be liable to the Gödel procedure for finding a formula unprovable-in-that-system. This formula the machine will be unable to produce as being true, although a mind can see that it is true. And so the machine will still not be an adequate model of the mind. We are trying to produce a model of the mind which is mechanical— which is essentially "dead"—but the mind, being in fact "alive," can always go one better than any formal, ossified, dead system can. Thanks to Gödel's theorem, the mind always has the last word.

A second objection will now be made. The procedure whereby the Gödelian formula is constructed is a standard procedure—only so could we be sure that a Gödelian formula can be constructed for every formal system. But if it is a standard procedure, then a machine should be able to be programed to carry it out too. We could construct a machine with the usual operations, and in addition an operation of going through the Gödel procedure, and then producing the conclusion of that procedure as being true; and then repeating the procedure, and so on, as often as required. This would correspond to having a system with an additional rule of inference which allowed one to add, as a theorem, the Gödelian formula of the rest of the formal system, and then the Gödelian formula of this new, strengthened, formal system, and so on. It would be tantamount to adding to the original formal system an infinite sequence of axioms, each the Gödelian formula of the system hitherto obtained. Yet even so, the matter is not settled: for the machine with a Gödelizing

operator, as we might call it, is a *different* machine from the machines
without such an operator; and, although the machine with the operator
would be able to do those things in which the machines without the
operator were outclassed by a mind, yet we might expect a mind, faced
with a machine that possessed a Gödelizing operator, to take this into
account, and out-Gödel the new machine, Gödelizing operator and all.
This has, in fact, proved to be the case. Even if we adjoin to a formal
system the infinite set of axioms consisting of the successive Gödelian
formulae, the resulting system is still incomplete, and contains a formula
which cannot be proved-in-the-system, although a rational being can,
standing outside the system, see that it is true.[2] We had expected this,
for even if an infinite set of axioms were added, they would have to be
specified by some finite rule or specification, and this further rule or
specification could then be taken into account by a mind considering the
enlarged formal system. In a sense, just because the mind has the last
word, it can always pick a hole in any formal system presented to it as
a model of its own workings. The mechanical model must be, in some
sense, finite and definite: and then the mind can always go one better.

   This is the answer to one objection put forward by Turing. He
argues that the limitation to the powers of a machine do not amount
to anything much. Although each individual machine is incapable of
getting the right answer to some questions, after all each individual
human being is fallible also: and in any case "our superiority can only
be felt on such an occasion in relation to the one machine over which
we have scored our petty triumph. There would be no question of triumphing simultaneously over *all* machines." But this is not the point.
We are not discussing whether machines or minds are superior, but
whether they are the same. In some respect machines are undoubtedly
superior to human minds; and the question on which they are stumped
is admittedly a rather niggling, even trivial, question. But it is enough,
enough to show that the machine is *not the same* as a mind. True, the
machine can do many things that a human mind cannot do: but if there
is of necessity something that the machine cannot do, though the mind
can, then, however trivial the matter is, we cannot equate the two, and
cannot hope ever to have a mechanical model that will adequately represent the mind. Nor does it signify that it is only an individual machine
we have triumphed over: for the triumph is not over only *an* individual
machine, but over *any* individual that anybody cares to specify—in Latin

---

[2] Gödel's original proof applies; see Secs. 1 and 6 init. of his lectures at the
Institute of Advanced Study, Princeton, N.J., 1934.

quivis or *quilibet,* not *quidam*—and a mechanical model of a mind must
be an individual machine. Although it is true that any particular "triumph" of a mind over a machine could be "trumped" by another machine able to produce the answer the first machine could not produce,
so that "there is no question of triumphing simultaneously over all
machines," yet this is irrelevant. What is at issue is not the unequal
contest between one mind and all machines, but whether there could be
any single machine that could do all a mind can do. For the mechanist
thesis to hold water, it must be possible, in principle, to produce a model,
a single model, which can do everything the mind can do. It is like a
game.[3] The mechanist has first turn. He produces *a—any,* but only a
definite one—mechanical model of the mind. I point to something that it
cannot do, but the mind can. The mechanist is free to modify his example, but each time he does so, I am entitled to look for defects in the
revised model. If the mechanist can devise a model that I cannot find
fault with, his thesis is established: if he cannot, then it is not proven:
and since—as it turns out—he necessarily cannot, it is refuted. To succeed, he must be able to produce some definite mechanical model of the
mind—any one he likes, but one he can specify, and will stick to. But
since he cannot, in principle cannot, produce any mechanical model that
is adequate, even though the point of failure is a minor one, he is bound
to fail, and mechanism must be false.

Deeper objections can still be made. Gödel's theorem applies to deductive systems, and human beings are not confined to making only deductive inferences. Gödel's theorem applies only to consistent systems, and
one may have doubts about how far it is permissible to assume that
human beings are consistent. Gödel's theorem applies only to formal
systems, and there is no a priori bound to human ingenuity which rules
out the possibility of our contriving some replica of humanity which was
not representable by a formal system.

Human beings are not confined to making deductive inferences, and
it has been urged by C. G. Hempel [4] and Hartley Rogers[5] that a fair
model of the mind would have to allow for the possibility of making
nondeductive inferences, and these might provide a way of escaping the
Gödel result. Hartley Rogers makes the specific suggestion that the

---

[3] For a similar type of argument, see two articles by the same author listed
in the bibliography at the end of this volume.

[4] In private conversation.

[5] *Theory of Recursive Functions, op. cit.*

machine should be programed to entertain various propositions which had not been proved or disproved, and on occasion to add them to its list of axioms. Fermat's last theorem or Goldbach's conjecture might thus be added. If subsequently their inclusion was found to lead to a contradiction, they would be dropped again, and indeed in those circumstances their negations would be added to the list of theorems. In this sort of way a machine might well be constructed which was able to produce as true certain formulae which could not be proved from its axioms according to its rules of inference. And therefore the method of demonstrating the mind's superiority over the machine might no longer work.

The construction of such a machine, however, presents difficulties. It cannot accept all unprovable formulae and add them to its axioms, or it will find itself accepting both the Gödelian formula and its negation, and so be inconsistent. Nor would it do if it accepted the first of each pair of undecidable formulae, and, having added that to its axioms, would no longer regard its negation as undecidable, and so would never accept it too: for it might happen on the wrong member of the pair: it might accept the negation of the Gödelian formula rather than the Gödelian formula itself. And the system constituted by a normal set of axioms with the negation of the Gödelian formula adjoined, although not inconsistent, is an unsound system, not admitting of the natural interpretation. It is something like non-Desarguian geometries in two dimensions: not actually inconsistent, but rather wrong, sufficiently much so to disqualify it from serious consideration. A machine which was liable to infelicities of that kind would be no model for the human mind.

It becomes clear that rather careful criteria of selection of unprovable formulae will be needed. Hartley Rogers suggests some possible ones. But once we have rules generating new axioms, even if the axioms generated are only provisionally accepted, and are liable to be dropped again if they are found to lead to inconsistency, then we can set about doing a Gödel on this system, as on any other. We are in the same case as when we had a rule generating the infinite set of Gödelian formulae as axioms. In short, however a machine is designed, it must proceed either at random or according to definite rules. Insofar as its procedure is random, we cannot outsmart it: but its performance is not going to be a convincing parody of intelligent behavior: insofar as its procedure is in accordance with definite rules, the Gödel method can be used to produce a formula which the machine, according to those rules, cannot assert as true, although we, standing outside the system, can see it to be true.[6]

Gödel's theorem applies only to consistent systems. All that we can prove *formally* is that *if* the system is consistent, then the Gödelian formula is unprovable-in-the-system. To be able to say categorically that the Gödelian formula is unprovable-in-the-system, and therefore true, we must not only be dealing with a consistent system, but be able to say that it is consistent. And, as Gödel showed in his second theorem—a corollary of his first—it is impossible to prove in a consistent system that that system is consistent. Thus in order to fault the machine by producing a formula of which we can say both that it is true and that the machine cannot produce it as true, we have to be able to say that the machine (or, rather, its corresponding formal system) is consistent; and there is no absolute proof of this. All we can do is to examine the machine and see if it appears consistent. There always remains the possibility of some inconsistency not yet detected. At best we can say that the machine is consistent, provided we are. But by what right can we do this? Gödel's second theorem seems to show that a man cannot assert his own consistency, and so Hartley Rogers[7] argues that we cannot really use Gödel's first theorem to counter the mechanist thesis unless we can say that "there are distinctive attributes which enable a human being to transcend this last limitation and assert his own consistency while still remaining consistent."

A man's untutored reaction if his consistency is questioned is to affirm it vehemently: but this, in view of Gödel's second theorem, is taken by some philosophers as evidence of his actual inconsistency. Professor Putnam[8] has suggested that human beings are machines, but inconsistent machines. If a machine were wired to correspond to an inconsistent system, then there would be no well-formed formula which it could not produce as true; and so in no way could it be proved to be inferior to a human being. Nor could we make its inconsistency a reproach to it—are not men inconsistent too? Certainly women are, and politicans; and

---

[6] Gödel's original proof applies if the rule is such as to generate a primitive recursive class of additional formulae; see Secs. 1 and 6 init. of his lectures at the Institute of Advanced Study. It is in fact sufficient that the class be recursively enumerable. See Barkley Rosser, "Extensions of Some Theorems of Gödel and Church," *Journal of Symbolic Logic,* Vol. I (1936), 87ff.

[7] *Op. cit.,* p. 154.

[8] In private conversation.

even male nonpoliticians contradict themselves sometimes, and a single inconsistency is enough to make a system inconsistent.

The fact that we are all sometimes inconsistent cannot be gainsaid, but from this it does not follow that we are tantamount to inconsistent systems. Our inconsistencies are mistakes rather than set policies. They correspond to the occasional malfunctioning of a machine, not its normal scheme of operations. Witness to this that we eschew inconsistencies when we recognize them for what they are. If we really were inconsistent machines, we should remain content with our inconsistencies, and would happily affirm both halves of a contradiction. Moreover, we would be prepared to say absolutely anything—which we are not. It is easily shown that in an inconsistent formal system everything is provable, and the requirement of consistency turns out to be just that not everything can be proved in it—it is not the case that "anything goes." This surely is a characteristic of the mental operations of human beings: they are selective: they do discriminate between favored—true—and unfavored—false—statements: when a person is prepared to say anything, and is prepared to contradict himself without any qualm or repugnance, then he is adjudged to have "lost his mind." Human beings, although not perfectly consistent, are not so much inconsistent as fallible.

A fallible but self-correcting machine would still be subject to Gödel's results. Only a fundamentally inconsistent machine would escape. Could we have a fundamentally inconsistent, but at the same time self-correcting machine, which both would be free of Gödel's results and yet would not be trivial and entirely unlike a human being? A machine with a rather *recherché* inconsistency wired into it, so that for all normal purposes it was consistent, but when presented with the Gödelian sentence was able to prove it?

There are all sorts of ways in which undesirable proofs might be obviated. We might have a rule that whenever we have proved p and not-p, we examine their proofs and reject the longer. Or we might arrange the axioms and rules of inference in a certain order, and when a proof leading to an inconsistency is proffered, see what axioms and rules are required for it, and reject that axiom or rule which comes last in the ordering. In some such way as this we could have an inconsistent system, with a stop-rule, so that the inconsistency was never allowed to come out in the form of an inconsistent formula.

The suggestion at first sight seems attractive: yet there is something deeply wrong. Even though we might preserve the façade of consistency

by having a rule that whenever two inconsistent formulae appear we
were to reject the one with the longer proof, yet such a rule would be
repugnant in our logical sense. Even the less arbitrary suggestions are
too arbitrary. No longer does the system operate with certain definite
rules of inference on certain definite formulae. Instead, the rules apply,
the axioms are true, provided . . . we do not happen to find it incon-
venient. We no longer know where we stand. One application of the
rule of Modus Ponens may be accepted while another is rejected: on
one occasion an axiom may be true, on another apparently false. The
system will have ceased to be a formal logical system, and the machine
will barely qualify for the title of a model for the mind. For it will be
far from resembling the mind in its operations: the mind does indeed
try out dubious axioms and rules of inference; but if they are found to
lead to contradiction, they are rejected altogether. We try out axioms
and rules of inference provisionally—true: but we do not keep them,
once they are found to lead to contradictions. We may seek to replace
them with others, we may feel that our formalization is at fault, and
that though some axiom or rule of inference of this sort its required, we
have not been able to formulate it quite correctly: but we do not retain
the faulty formulations without modification, merely with the proviso
that when the argument leads to a contradiction we refuse to follow it.
To do this would be utterly irrational. We should be in the position
that on some occasions when supplied with the premises of a Modus
Ponens, say, we applied the rule and allowed the conclusion, and on
other occasions we refused to apply the rule, and disallowed the conclusion. A person, or a machine, which did this without being able to give
a good reason for so doing, would be accounted arbitrary and irrational.
It is part of the concept of "arguments" or "reasons" that they are in
some sense general and universal: that if Modus Ponens is a valid
method of arguing when I am establishing a desired conclusion, it is a
valid method also when you, my opponent, are establishing a conclusion
I do not want to to accept. We cannot pick and choose the times when
a form of argument is to be valid; not if we are to be reasonable. It is
of course true, that with our informal arguments, which are not fully
formalized, we do distinguished between arguments which are at first
sight similar, adding further reasons why they are nonetheless not really
similar: and it might be maintained that a machine might likewise be
entitled to distinguish between arguments at first sight similar, if it had
good reason for doing so. And it might further be maintained that the

machine had good reason for rejecting those patterns of argument it did reject, indeed the best of reasons, namely the avoidance of contradiction. But that, if it is a reason at all, is too good a reason. We do not lay it to a man's credit that he avoids contradiction merely by refusing to accept those arguments which would lead him to it, for no other reason than that otherwise he would be led to it. Special pleading rather than sound argument is the name for that type of reasoning. No credit accrues to a man who, clever enough to see a few moves of argument ahead, avoids being brought to acknowledge his own inconsistency, by stonewalling as soon as he sees where the argument will end. Rather, we account him inconsistent too, not, in his case, because he affirmed and denied the same proposition, but because he used and refused to use the same rule of inference. A stop-rule on actually enunciating an inconsistency is not enough to save an inconsistent machine from being called inconsistent.

The possibility yet remains that we are inconsistent, and there is no stop-rule, but the inconsistency is so *recherché* that it has never turned up. After all, *naïve* set-theory, which was deeply embedded in common-sense ways of thinking did turn out to be inconsistent. Can we be sure that a similar fate is not in store for simple arithmetic too? In a sense we cannot, in spite of our great feeling of certitude that our system of whole numbers which can be added and multiplied together is never going to prove inconsistent. It is just conceivable we might find we had formalized it incorrectly. If we had, we should try and formulate anew our intuitive concept of number, as we have our intuitive concept of a set. If we did this, we should of course recast our system: our present axioms and rules of inference would be utterly rejected: there would be no question of our using and not using them in an "inconsistent" fashion. We should, once we had recast the system, be in the same position as we are now, possessed of a system believed to be consistent, but not provably so. But then could there not be some other inconsistency? It is indeed a possibility. But again no inconsistency once detected will be tolerated. We are determined not to be inconsistent, and are resolved to root out inconsistency, should any appear. Thus, although we can never be completely certain or completely free of the risk of having to think out our mathematics again, the ultimate position must be one of two: either we have a system of simple arithmetic which to the best of our knowledge and belief is consistent: or there is no such system possible. In the former case we are in the same position as at present: in the latter, if we find that no system containing simple arithmetic can be free of contradictions, we shall have to abandon not merely the whole of mathematics and the mathematical sciences, but the whole of thought.

It may still be maintained that although a man must in this sense assume, he cannot properly affirm, his own consistency without thereby belying his words. We may be consistent; indeed we have every reason to hope that we are: but a necessary modesty forbids us from saying so. Yet this is not quite what Gödel's second theorem states. Gödel has shown that in a consistent system a formula stating the consistency of the system cannot be proved *in that system*. It follows that a machine, if consistent, cannot produce as true an assertion of its own consistency: hence also that a mind, *if it were really a machine,* could not reach the conclusion that it was a consistent one. For a mind which is not a machine no such conclusion follows. All that Gödel has proved is that a mind cannot produce a formal proof of the consistency of a formal system inside the system itself: but there is no objection to going outside the system and no objection to producing informal arguments for the consistency either of a formal system or of something less formal and less systematized. Such informal arguments will not be able to be completely formalized: but then the whole tenor of Gödel's results is that we ought not to ask, and cannot obtain, complete formalization. And although it would have been nice if we could have obtained them, since completely formalized arguments are more coercive than informal ones, yet since we cannot have all our arguments cast into that form, we must not hold it against informal arguments that they are informal or regard them all as utterly worthless. It therefore seems to me both proper and reasonable for a mind to assert its own consistency: proper, because although machines, as we might have expected, are unable to reflect fully on their own performance and powers, yet to be able to be self-conscious in this way is just what we expect of minds: and reasonable, for the reasons given. Not only can we fairly say simply that we *know* we are consistent, apart from our mistakes, but we must in any case *assume* that we are, if thought is to be possible at all; moreover we are selective, we will not, as inconsistent machines would, say anything and everything whatsoever: and finally we can, in a sense, *decide* to be consistent, in the sense that we can resolve not to tolerate inconsistencies in our thinking and speaking, and to eliminate them, if ever they should appear, by withdrawing and cancelling one limb of the contradiction.

We can see how we might almost have expected Gödel's theorem to distinguish self-conscious beings from inanimate objects. The essence of the Gödelian formula is that it is self-referring. It says that "This formula is unprovable-in-this-system." When carried over to a machine, the formula is specified in terms which depend on the particular machine in question. The machine is being asked a question about its own processes. We are asking it to be self-conscious, and say what things it can and cannot do. Such questions notoriously lead to paradox. At one's first and simplest attempts to philosophize, one becomes entangled in questions of whether when one knows something one knows that one knows it, and what, when one is thinking of oneself, is being thought about, and what is doing the thinking. After one has been puzzled and bruised by this problem for a long time, one learns not to press these questions: the concept of a conscious being is, implicitly, realized to be different from that of an unconscious object. In saying that a conscious being knows something, we are saying not only that he knows it, but that he knows that he knows it, and that he knows that he knows that he knows it, and so on, as long as we care to pose the question: there is, we recognize, an infinity here, but it is not an infinite regress in the bad sense, for it is the questions that peter out, as being pointless, rather than the answers. The questions are felt to be pointless because the concept contains within itself the idea of being able to go on answering such questions indefinitely. Although conscious beings have the power of going on, we do not wish to exhibit this simply as a succession of tasks they are able to perform, nor do we see the mind as an infinite sequence of selves and super-selves and super-super-selves. Rather, we insist that a conscious being is a unity, and though we talk about parts of the mind, we do so only as a metaphor, and will not allow it to be taken literally.

The paradoxes of consciousness arise because a conscious being can be aware of itself, as well as of other things, and yet cannot really be construed as being divisible into parts. It means that a conscious being can deal with Gödelian questions in a way in which a machine cannot, because a conscious being can both consider itself and its performance and yet not be other than that which did the performance. A machine can be made in a manner of speaking to "consider" its own performance, but it cannot take this "into account" without thereby becoming a different machine, namely the old machine with a "new part" added. But it is inherent in our idea of a conscious mind that it can reflect upon itself and criticize its own performances, and no extra part is required to do this: it is already complete, and has no Achilles' heel.

The thesis thus begins to become more a matter of conceptual analysis than mathematical discovery. This is borne out by considering another argument put forward by Turing. So far, we have constructed only fairly simple and predictable artifacts. When we increase the complexity of our machines there may, perhaps, be surprises in store for us. He draws a parallel with a fission pile. Below a certain "critical" size, nothing much happens: but above the critical size, the sparks begin to fly. So too, perhaps, with brains and machines. Most brains and all machines are, at present, "sub-critical"—they react to incoming stimuli in a stodgy and uninteresting way, have no ideas of their own, can produce only stock responses—but a few brains at present, and possibly some machines in the future, are super-critical, and scintillate on their own account. Turing is suggesting that it is only a matter of complexity, and that above a certain level of complexity a qualitative difference appears, so that "super-critical" machines will be quite unlike the simple ones hitherto envisaged.

This may be so. Complexity often does introduce qualitative differences. Although it sounds implausible, it might turn out that above a certain level of complexity, a machine ceased to be predictable, even in principle, and started doing things on its own account, or, to use a very revealing phrase, it might begin to have a mind of its own. It might begin to have a mind of its own. It would begin to have a mind of its own when it was no longer entirely predictable and entirely docile, but was capable of doing things which we recognized as intelligent, and not just mistakes or random shots, but which we had not programed into it. But then it would cease to be a machine, within the meaning of the act. What is at stake in the mechanist debate is not how minds are, or might be, brought into being, but how they operate. It is essential for the mechanist thesis that the mechanical model of the mind shall operate according to "mechanical principles," that is, that we can understand the operation of the whole in terms of the operations of its parts, and the operation of each part either shall be determined by its initial state and the construction of the machine, or shall be a random choice between a determinate number of determinate operations. If the mechanist produces a machine which is so complicated that this ceases to hold good of it, then it is no longer a machine for the purposes of our discussion, no matter how it was constructed. We should say, rather, that he had created a mind, in the same sort of sense as we procreate people at present. There would then be two ways of bringing new minds into the world, the traditional way, by begetting children born of women, and a new way by constructing very, very complicated systems of, say, valves and relays. When talking of the second way, we should take care to stress that although what was created looked like a machine, it was not one really, because it was not just the total of its parts. One could not tell what it was going to do merely by knowing the way in which it was built up and the initial state of its parts: one could not even tell the limits of what it could do, for even when presented with a Gödel-type question, it got the answer right. In fact we should say briefly that any system which was not floored by the Gödel question was *eo ipso* not a Turing machine, i.e., not a machine within the meaning of the act.

If the proof of the falsity of mechanism is valid, it is of the greatest consequence for the whole of philosophy. Since the time of Newton, the bogey of mechanist determinism has obsessed philosophers. If we were to be scientific, it seemed that we must look on human beings as determined automata, and not as autonomous moral agents; if we were to be moral, it seemed that we must deny science its due, set an arbitrary limit to its progress in understanding human neurophysiology, and take refuge in obscurantist mysticism. Not even Kant could resolve the tension between the two standpoints. But now, though many arguments against human freedom still remain, the argument from mechanism, perhaps the most compelling argument of them all, has lost its power. No longer on this count will it be incumbent on the natural philosopher to deny freedom in the name of science: no longer will the moralist feel the urge to abolish knowledge to make room for faith. We can even begin to see how there could be room for morality, without its being necessary to abolish or even to circumscribe the province of science. Our argument has set no limits to scientific inquiry: it will still be possible to investigate the working of the brain. It will still be possible to produce mechanical models of the mind. Only, now we can see that no mechanical model will be completely adequate, nor any explanations in purely mechanist terms. We can produce models and explanations, and they will be illuminating: but, however far they go, there will always remain more to be said. There is no arbitrary bound to scientific inquiry: but no scientific inquiry can ever exhaust the infinite variety of the human mind.

THE IMITATION GAME

KEITH GUNDERSON

I

Disturbed by what he took to be the ambiguous, if not meaningless, character of the question "Can machines think?," the late A. M. Turing in his article "Computing Machinery and Intelligence" [see above] sought to replace that question in the following way. He said:

> The new form of the problem can be described in terms of a game which we call the "imitation game." It is played with three people, a man (A), a woman (B), and an interrogator (C) who may be either sex. The interrogator stays in a room apart from the other two. The object of the game for the interrogator is to determine which of the other two is the man and which is the woman. He knows them by labels X and Y, and at the end of the game he says either "X is A and Y is B" or "X is B and Y is A." The interrogator is allowed to put questions to A and B thus:
>
> C: "Will X please tell me the length of his or her hair?"

"The Imitation Game," forthcoming in Mind. *Reprinted by permission of the author and the editor of* Mind.

Now suppose X is actually A, then A must answer. It is A's object in the game to try to cause C to make the wrong identification. His answer might therefore be

"My hair is shingled, and the longest strands are about nine inches long."

In order that tones of voice may not help the interrogator the answers should be written, or better still, typewritten. The ideal arrangement is to have a teleprinter communicating between the two rooms. Alternatively the question and answers can be repeated by an intermediary. The object of the game for the third player (B) is to help the interrogator. The best strategy for her is probably to give truthful answers. She can add such things as "I am the woman, don't listen to him!" to her answers, but it will avail nothing as the man can make similar remarks.

We now ask the question, "What will happen when a machine takes the part of A in this game?" Will the interrogator decide wrongly as often as when the game is played between a man and a woman? These questions replace our original, "Can machines think?"

And Turing's answers to these latter questions are more or less summed up in the following passage: "I believe that in fifty years' time it will be possible to program computers, with a storage capacity of about 10^9, to make them play the imitation game so well that an average interrogator will not have more than 70 per cent chance of making the right identification after five minutes of questioning." And though he goes on to reiterate that he suspects that the original question "Can machines think?" is meaningless, and that it should be disposed of and replaced by a more precise formulation of the problems involved (a formulation such as a set of questions about the imitation game and machine capacities), what finally emerges is that Turing does answer the "meaningless" question after all, and that his answer is in the affirmative and follows from his conclusions concerning the capabilities of machines which might be successfully substituted for people in the imitation-game context.

It should be pointed out that Turing's beliefs about the possible capabilities and capacities of machines are not limited to such activities as playing the imitation game as successfully as human beings. He does not, for example, deny that it might be possible to develop a machine which would relish the taste of strawberries and cream, though he thinks it would be "idiotic" to attempt to make one, and confines himself on the whole in his positive account to considerations of machine capacities which could be illustrated in terms of playing the imitation game.

So we shall be primarily concerned with asking whether or not a machine, which could play the imitation game as well as Turing thought it might, would thus be a machine which we would have good reasons for saying was capable of thought and what would be involved in saying this.

Some philosophers[1] have not been satisfied with Turing's treatment of the question "Can machines think?" But the imitation game itself, which indeed seems to constitute the hub of his positive treatment, has been little more than alluded to or remarked on in passing. I shall try to develop in a somewhat more detailed way certain objections to it, objections which, I believe, Turing altogether fails to anticipate. My remarks shall thus in the main be critically oriented, which is not meant to suggest that I believe there are no plausible lines of defense open to a supporter of Turing. I shall, to the contrary, close with a brief attempt to indicate what some of these might be and some general challenges which I think Turing has raised for the philosopher of mind. But these latter I shall not elaborate upon.

II

Let us consider the following question: "Can rocks imitate?" One might say that it is a question "too meaningless to deserve discussion." Yet it seems possible to reformulate the problem in relatively unambiguous words as follows:

> The new form of the problem can be described in terms of a game which we call the "toe-stepping game." It is played with three people, a man (A), a woman (B), and an interrogator (C) who may be of either sex. The interrogator stays in a room apart from the other two. The door is closed, but there is a small opening in the wall next to the floor through which he can place most of his foot. When he does so, one of the other two may step on his toe. The object of the game for the interrogator is to determine, by the way in which his toe is stepped on, which of the other two is the man and which is the woman. He knows them by labels X and Y, and at the end of the game he says either "X is A and Y is B" or "X is B and Y is A." Now the interrogator—rather the person whose toe gets stepped on—may indicate before he puts

---

[1] See Michael Scriven, "The Mechanical Concept of Mind," pp. 31ff., and "The Compleat Robot: A Prolegomena to Androidology" in *Dimensions of Mind*, Sidney Hook, ed. (New York: New York University Press, 1960). Also a remark by Paul Ziff in "The Feelings of Robots," pp. 98ff., and others—for example, C. E. Shannon and J. McCarthy in their preface to *Automata Studies* (Princeton: Princeton University Press, 1956).

his foot through the opening, whether X or Y is to step on it. Better yet, there might be a narrow division in the opening, one side for X and one for Y (one for A and one for B).

Now suppose C puts his foot through A's side of the opening (which may be labeled X or Y on C's side of the wall). It is A's object in the game to try to cause C to make the wrong identification. His step on the toe might therefore be quick and jabbing like some high-heeled woman.

The object of the game for the third player (B) is to help the person whose toe gets stepped on. The best strategy for her is probably to try to step on it in the most womanly way possible. She can add such things as a slight twist of a high heel to her stepping, but it will avail nothing as the man can step in similar ways, since he will also have at his disposal various shoes with which to vary his toe-stepping.

We now ask the question: "What will happen when a rock-box (a box filled with rocks of varying weights, sizes, and shapes) is constructed with an electric eye which operates across the opening in the wall so that it releases a rock which descends upon C's toe whenever C puts his foot through A's side of the opening, and thus comes to take the part of A in this game?" (The situation can be made more convincing by constructing the rock-box so that there is a mechanism pulling up the released rock shortly after its descent, thus avoiding telltale noises such as a rock rolling on the floor, etc.) Will then the interrogator—the person whose toe gets stepped on—decide wrongly as often as when the game is played between a man and a woman? These questions replace our original, "Can rocks imitate?"

I believe that in less than fifty years' time it will be possible to set up elaborately constructed rock-boxes, with large rock-storage capacities, so that they will play the toe-stepping game so well that the average person who would get his toe stepped on would not have more than 70 per cent chance of making the right identification after about five minutes of toe-stepping.

The above seems to show the following: what follows from the toe-stepping game situation surely is not that rocks are able to imitate (I assume no one would want to take that path of argument) but only that they are able to be rigged in such a way that they could be substituted for a human being in a toe-stepping game without changing any essential characteristics of that game. And this is claimed in spite of the fact that if a human being were to play the toe-stepping game as envisaged above, we would no doubt be correct in saying that that person was imitating, etc. To be sure, a digital computer is a more august mechanism than a rock-box, but Turing has not provided us with any arguments for believing that its role in the imitation game, as distinct from the net results it yields, is any closer a match for a human being executing such a role, than is the rock-box's execution of its role in the toe-stepping game a match for a human being's execution of a similar role. The parody comparison can be pushed too far. But I think it lays bare the reason why there is no contradiction involved in saying, "Yes, a machine can play the imitation game, but it can't think." It is for the same reason that there is no contradiction in saying, "Of course a rock-box of such-and-such a sort can be set up, but rocks surely can't imitate." For thinking (or imitating) cannot be fully described simply by pointing to net results such as those illustrated above. For if this were not the case it would be correct to say that a piece of chalk could think or compose because it was freakishly blown about by a tornado in such a way that it scratched a rondo on a blackboard, and that a phonograph could sing, and that an electric-eye could see people coming.

People may be let out of a building by either an electric-eye or a doorman. The end result is the same. But though a doorman may be rude or polite, the electric-eye neither practices nor neglects etiquette. Turing brandishes net results. But I think the foregoing at least indicates certain difficulties with any account of thinking or decision as to whether a certain thing is capable of thought which is based primarily on net results. And, of course, one could always ask whether the net results were really the same. But I do not wish to follow that line of argument here. It is my main concern simply to indicate where Turing's account, which is cast largely in terms of net results, fails because of this. It is not an effective counter to reply: "But part of the net results in question includes intelligent people being deceived!" For what would this add to the general argument? No doubt people could be deceived by rock-boxes! It is said that hi-fidelity phonographs have been perfected to the point where blindfolded music critics are unable to distinguish their "playing" from that of, let us say, the Budapest String Quartet. But the phonograph would never be said to have performed with unusual brilliance on Saturday, nor would it ever deserve an encore.

III

Now perhaps comparable net results achieved by machines and human beings is all that is needed to establish an analogy between them, but it is far from what is needed to establish that one sort of subject (machines) can do the same thing that another sort of subject (human beings or other animals) can do. Part of what things do is how they do it. To ask whether a machine can think is in part to ask whether machines can do things in certain ways.

The above is relevant to what might be called the problem of distinguishing and evaluating the net results achieved by a machine as it is touched on by Scriven in his discussion of what he calls "the performatory problem" and "the personality problem." In "The Compleat Robot: A Prolegomena to Androidology," [see bibliography] he writes:

> The performatory problem here is whether a computer can produce results which, when translated, provide what would count as an original solution or proof *if it came from a man.* The personality problem is whether we are entitled to call such a result a solution or proof, despite the fact that it did *not* come from a man.

And continues:

> The logical trap is this: no *one* performatory achievement will be enough to persuade us to apply the human-achievement vocabulary, but if we refuse to use this vocabulary in each case separately, on this ground, we will, perhaps wrongly, have committed ourselves to avoiding it even when *all* the achievements are simultaneously attained.

My concern is not, however, with what is to count as an original solution or proof. Scriven, in the above, is commenting on the claims: "Machines only do what we tell them to do. They are incapable of genuinely original thought." He says that two "importantly different points are run together." The above is his attempt to separate these points. But it seems that there are at least three, and not just two, points which are run together in the just-mentioned claims. The third point, the one not covered by Scriven's distinction between the performatory and personality problems, is simply the problem, mentioned above, of discerning when one subject (a machine) has *done the same thing* as another subject (a human being). And here "doing the same thing" does not simply mean "achieved similar end result." (Which is not to suggest that the phrase can never be used in that way in connection with thinking.) This is of interest in respect to Scriven's discussion, since it might be the case that all the achievements were simultaneously attained by a machine, as Scriven suggests, and that we had decided on various grounds that they should count as original proofs and solutions and thus surmounted the personality problem, but yet felt unwilling to grant that the machines were capable of "genuinely original thought." Our grounds for this latter decision might be highly parallel to our grounds for not wanting to say that rocks could imitate (even though rock-boxes had reached a high level of development). Of course our grounds might not be as sound as these. I am simply imagining the case where they are, which is also a case where all the achievements are attained in such a way that they count as original solutions or proofs. In this case we would see that answers to questions about originality and performance and the logical trap mentioned by Scriven would be wholly separate from whatever answers might be given to the question whether or not the machines involved thought, and would thus be unsuitable as answers to the question whether or not they were capable of "genuinely original thought." In other words, questions as to originality and questions as to thinking are not the same, but this dissimilarity is left unacknowledged in Scriven's account.

IV

But let us return to the imitation game itself. It is to be granted that if human beings were to participate in such a game, we would almost surely regard them as deliberating, deciding, wondering—in short, "thinking things over"—as they passed their messages back and forth. And if someone were to ask us for an example of Johnson's intellectual prowess or mental capabilities, we might well point to this game which he often played, and how he enjoyed trying to outwit Peterson and Hanson who also participated in it. But we would only regard it as one of the many examples we might give of Peterson's mental capacities. We would ordinarily not feel hard pressed to produce countless other examples of Peterson deliberating, figuring, wondering, reflecting, or what in short we can call thinking. We might, for example, relate how he works over his sonnets or how he argues with Hanson. Now, I do not want to deny that it is beyond the scope of a machine to do these latter things. I am not, in fact, here concerned with giving an answer to the question, "Can machines think?" What I instead want to emphasize is that what we would say about Peterson in countless other situations is bound to influence what we say about him in the imitation game. A rock rolls down a hill and there is, strictly speaking, no behavior or action on the part of the rock. But if a man rolls down a hill we might well ask if he was pushed or did it intentionally, whether he's enjoying himself, playing a game, pretending to be a tumbleweed, or what. We cannot think of a man as simply or purely rolling down a hill—unless he is dead. A fortiori, we cannot understand him being a participant in the imitation game apart from his dispositions, habits, etc., which are exhibited in contexts other than the imitation game. Thus we cannot hope to find any decisive answer to the question as to how we should characterize a machine which can play (well) the imitation game, by asking what we would say about a man who could play (well) the imitation game. Thinking, whatever positive characterization or account is correct, is not something which any one example will explain or decide. But the part of Turing's case which I've been concerned with rests largely on one example.

V

The following might help to clarify the above. Imagine the dialogue below:

Vacuum Cleaner Salesman: Now here's an example of what the all-purpose Swish 600 can do. (He then applies the nozzle to the carpet and it sucks up a bit of dust.)

Housewife: What else can it do?

Vacuum Cleaner Salesman: What do you mean "What else can it do?" It just sucked up that bit of dust, didn't you see?

Housewife: Yes, I saw it suck up a bit of dust, but I thought it was all-purpose. Doesn't it suck up larger and heavier bits of straw or paper or mud? And can't it get in the tight corners? Doesn't it have other nozzles? What about the cat hair on the couch?

Vacuum Cleaner Salesman: It sucks up bits of dust. That's what vacuum cleaners are for.

Housewife: Oh, that's what it does. I thought it was simply an example of what it does.

Vacuum Cleaner Salesman: It is an example of what it does. What it does is to suck up bits of dust.

We ask: Who's right about examples? We answer: It's not perfectly clear that anyone is lying or unjustifiably using the word "example." And there's no obvious linguistic rule or regularity to point to which tells us that if S can only do x, then S's doing x cannot be an example of what S can do since being an example presupposes or entails or what-not that other kinds of examples are forthcoming (sucking up mud, cat hair, etc.). Yet, in spite of this, the housewife has a point. One simply has a right to expect more from an all-purpose Swish 600 than what has been demonstrated. Here clearly the main trouble is with "all-purpose" rather than with "example," though there may still be something misleading about saying, "Here's an example . . . ," and it would surely mislead to say, "Here's *just* an example . . . ," followed by ". . . of what the all-purpose Swish 600 can do." The philosophical relevance of all this to our own discussion can be put in the following rather domestic way: "thinking" is a term which shares certain features with "all-purpose" as it occurs in the phrase "all-purpose Swish 600." It is not used to designate or refer to one capability, capacity, disposition, talent, habit, or feature of a given subject any more than "all-purpose" in the above example is used to mark out one particular operation of a vacuum cleaner. Thinking, whatever positive account one might give of it, is not, for example, like swimming or tennis playing. The question as to whether Peterson can swim or play tennis can be settled by a few token examples of Peterson swimming or playing tennis. (And it might be noted it is hardly imaginable that the question as to whether Peterson could think or not would be raised. For in general it is not at all interesting to ask that question of contemporary human beings, though it might be interesting for contemporary human beings to raise it in connection with different anthropoids viewed at various stages of their evolution.) But if we suppose the question were raised in connection with Peterson the only appropriate sort of answer to it would be one like, "Good heavens, what makes you think he can't?" (as if anticipating news of some horrible brain injury inflicted on Peterson). And our shock would not be at his perhaps having lost a particular talent. It would not be like the case of a Wimbledon champion losing his tennis talent because of an amputated arm.

It is no more unusual for a human being to be capable of thought than it is for a human being to be composed of cells. Similarly, "He can think" is no more an answer to questions concerning Peterson's mental capacities or intelligence, than "He's composed of cells" is an answer to the usual type of question about Peterson's appearance. And to say that Peterson can think is not to say there are a few token examples of thinking which are at our fingertips, any more than to say that the Swish 600 is all-purpose is to have in mind a particular maneuver or two of which the device is capable. It is because thinking cannot be identified with what can be shown by any one example or type of example; thus Turing's approach to the question "Can a machine think?" via the imitation game is less than convincing. In effect he provides us below with a dialogue very much like the one above:

Turing: You know, machines can think.

Philosopher: Good heavens! Really? How do you know?

Turing: Well, they can play what's called the imitation game. (This is followed by a description of same.)

Philosopher: Interesting. What else can they do? They must be capable of a great deal if they can really think.

Turing: What do you mean, "What else can they do?" They play the imitation game. That's thinking, isn't it?

Etc.

But Turing, like the vacuum cleaner salesman, has trouble making his sale. Nonetheless, I will indicate shortly why certain of our criticisms of his approach might have to be modified.

VI

But one last critical remark before pointing to certain shortcomings of the foregoing. As indicated before, Turing's argument benefits from his emphasizing the fact that a machine is being substituted for a human being in a certain situation, and does as well as a human being would do in that situation. No one, however, would want to deny that machines are able to do a number of things as well as or more competently than human beings, though surely no one would want to say that every one of such examples provided further arguments in support of the claim that machines can think. For in many such cases one might, instead of emphasizing that a machine can do what a human being can do, emphasize that one hardly needs to be a human being to do such things. For example: "I don't even have to think at my job; I just seal the jars as they move along the belt," or, "I just pour out soft drinks one after the other like some machine." The latter could hardly be construed as suggesting "My, aren't soft-drink vending machines clever," but rather suggests, "Isn't my job stupid; it involves little or no mental effort at all." Furthermore, as Professor Ryle has suggested to me, a well-trained bank cashier can add, subtract, multiply, and divide without having to think about what he is doing and while thinking about something else, and can't many of us run through the alphabet or a popular song without thinking? This is not meant to be a specific criticism of Turing as much as it is meant as a reminder that being able to do what human beings can do hardly implies the presence of intellectual or mental skills real or simulated, since so many things which human beings do involve little if any thinking. Those without jobs constitute a somewhat different segment of the population from those without wits.

VII

But the following considerations seem to temper some of the foregoing criticisms. A defender of Turing might emphasize that a machine
that is able to play the imitation game is also able to do much more:
it can compute, perhaps be programed to play chess, etc., and consequently displays capacities far beyond the "one example" which has been
emphasized in our criticisms. I shall not go into the details which I
think an adequate reply to this challenge must take into account. But
in general I believe it would be possible to formulate a reply along the
lines that would show that even playing chess, calculating, and the performance of other (most likely computational) operations provide us
with at best a rather narrow range of examples and still fails to satisfy
our intuitive concept of thinking. The parallel case in respect to the
Housewife and Vacuum Cleaner Salesman would be where the Housewife still refused to accept the vacuum cleaner as "all-purpose" even
though it had been shown to be capable of picking up scraps somewhat
heavier than dust. Nonetheless, even if our reply were satisfactory, the
more general question would remain unanswered: what range of examples would satisfy the implicit criteria we use in our ordinary characterization of subjects as "those capable of thought"?

A corollary: If we are to keep the question "Can machines think?"
interesting, we cannot withhold a positive answer simply on the grounds
that it (a machine) does not duplicate human activity in every respect.
The question "Can a machine think if it can do everything a human
being can do?" is not an interesting question, though it is somewhat
interesting to ask whether there would not be a logical contradiction
in supposing such to be, in fact, a machine. But as long as we have in
mind subjects which obviously are machines, we must be willing to stop
short of demanding their activities to fully mirror human ones before
we say they can think, if they can. But how far short? Again the above
question as to the variety and extent of examples required is raised.

Furthermore, it might be asserted that with the increasing role of
machines in society the word "think" itself might take on new meanings, and that it is not unreasonable to suppose it changing in meaning
in such a way that fifty years hence a machine which could play the
imitation game would in ordinary parlance be called a machine which
could think. There is, however, a difference between asking whether a
machine can think given current meanings and uses of "machine" and

"think" and asking whether a machine can think given changes in the meanings of "machine" and "think." My own attention has throughout this paper been centered on the first question. Yet there is a temporal obscurity in the question "Can machines think?" For if the question is construed as ranging over possible futures, it may be difficult to discuss such futures without reference to changing word meanings and uses. But this raises an entire family of issues which there is not space to discuss here. To some extent Turing's own views are based on certain beliefs he has about how we will in the future talk about machines. But these are never discussed in any detail, and he does not address himself to the knotty problems of meaning which interlace with them.

VIII

A final point: the stance is often taken that thinking is the crowning capacity or achievement of the human race, and that if one denies that machines can think, one in effect assigns them to some lower level of achievement than that attained by human beings. But one might well contend that machines can't think, for they do much better than that. We could forever deny that a machine could think through a mathematical problem, and still claim that in many respects the achievement of machines was on a higher level than that attained by thinking beings, since machines can almost instantaneously and infallibly produce accurate and sometimes original answers to many complex and difficult mathematical problems with which they are presented. They do not need to "think out" the answers. In the end the steam drill outlasted John Henry as a digger of railway tunnels, but that didn't prove the machine had muscles; it proved that muscles were not needed for digging railway tunnels.

MINDS AND MACHINES

HILARY PUTNAM

The various issues and puzzles that make up the traditional mind-body problem are wholly linguistic and logical in character: whatever few empirical "facts" there may be in this area support one view as much as another. I do not hope to establish this contention in this paper, but I hope to do something toward rendering it more plausible. Specifically, I shall try to show that all of the issues arise in connection with any computing system capable of answering questions about its own structure, and have thus nothing to do with the unique nature (if it *is* unique) of human subjective experience.

To illustrate the sort of thing that is meant: one kind of puzzle that is sometimes discussed in connection with the "mind-body problem" is the puzzle of *privacy*. The question "How do I know I have a pain?"

"Minds and Machines," Dimensions of Mind: A Symposium, *Sidney Hook, ed. (New York: New York University Press, 1960). Reprinted by permission of the author and New York University Press.*

is a *deviant*[1] ("logically odd") question. The question "How do I know Smith has a pain?" is not at all deviant. The difference can also be mirrored in impersonal questions: "How does anyone ever know he himself has a pain?" is deviant; "How does anyone ever know that someone else is in pain?" is nondeviant. I shall show that the difference in status between the last two questions is mirrored in the case of machines: if T is any *Turing machine* (see below), the question "How does T ascertain that it is in state A?" is, as we shall see, "logically odd" with a vengeance; but if T is capable of investigating its neighbor machine T' (say, T has electronic "sense organs" which "scan" T'), the question "How does T ascertain that T' is in state A?" is not at all odd.

Another question connected with the "mind-body problem" is the question whether or not it is ever permissible to identify mental events and physical events. Of course, I do not claim that this question arises for Turing machines, but I do claim that it is possible to construct a logical analogue for this question that does arise, and that all of the arguments on both sides of the question of "mind-body identity" can be mirrored in terms of the analogue.

To obtain such an analogue, let us identify a scientific theory with a "partially interpreted calculus" in the sense of Carnap.[2] Then we can perfectly well imagine a Turing machine which generates theories, tests them (assuming that it is possible to "mechanize" inductive logic to some degree), and "accepts" theories which satisfy certain criteria (e.g., predictive success). In particular, if the machine has electronic "sense organs" which enable it to "scan" itself while it is in operation, it may formulate theories concerning its own structure and subject them to test. Suppose the machine is in a given state (say, "state A") when, and only when, flip-flop 36 is on. Then this statement: "I am in state A when, and only when, flip-flop 36 is on," may be one of the theoretical principles concerning its own structure accepted by the machine. Here

---

[1] By a "deviant" utterance is here meant one that deviates from a semantical regularity (in the appropriate natural language). The term is taken from Paul Ziff, *Semantic Analysis* (Ithaca, N.Y.: Cornell University Press, 1960).

[2] Cf. Rudolf Carnap, "The Interpretation of Physics," in *Readings in the Philosophy of Science,* H. Feigl and M. Brodbeck, eds. (New York: Appleton-Century-Crofts, Inc., 1953), and "The Methodological Character of Theoretical Concepts," in *Foundations of Science and the Concepts of Psychology and Psychoanalysis,* H. Feigl and M. Scriven, eds., Minnesota Studies in the Philosophy of Science, Vol. I (Minneapolis: University of Minnesota Press, 1956). This model of a scientific theory is too oversimplified to be of much general utility, in my opinion: however, the oversimplifications do not affect the present argument.

"I am in state A" is, of course, "observation language" for the machine, while "flip-flop 36 is on" is a "theoretical expression" which is partially interpreted in terms of "observables" (if the machine's "sense organs" report by printing symbols on the machine's input tape, the "observables" in terms of which the machine would give a partial operational defini- tion of "flip-flop 36 being on" would be of the form "symbol # so- and-so appearing on the input tape"). Now all of the usual considera- tions for and against mind-body identification can be paralleled by con- siderations for and against saying that state A is in fact *identical* with flip-flop 36 being on.

Corresponding to Occamist arguments for "identity" in the one case are Occamist arguments for identity in the other. And the usual argu- ment for dualism in the mind-body case can be paralleled in the other as follows: for the machine, "state A" is directly observable; on the other hand, "flip-flops" are something it knows about only via highly sophisticated inferences— How *could* two things so different *possibly* be the same?

This last argument can be put into a form which makes it appear somewhat stronger. The proposition:

(1) I am in state A if, and only if, flip-flop 36 is on,

is clearly a "synthetic" proposition for the machine. For instance, the machine might be in state A and its sense organs might report that flip- flop 36 was *not* on. In such a case the machine would have to make a methodological "choice"—namely, to give up (1) or to conclude that it had made an "observational error" (just as a human scientist would be confronted with similar methodological choices in studying his own psychophysical correlations). And just as philosophers have argued from the synthetic nature of the proposition:

(2) I am in pain if, and only if, my C-fibers are stimulated,

to the conclusion that the *properties* (or "states" or "events") being in pain, and having C-fibers stimulated, cannot possibly be the same [other- wise (2) would be analytic, or so the argument runs]; so one should be able to conclude from the fact that (1) is synthetic that the two prop- erties (or "states" or "events")—being in state A and having flip-flop 36 on—cannot possibly be the same!

It is instructive to note that the traditional argument for dualism is not at all a conclusion from "the raw data of direct experience" (as is shown by the fact that it applies just as well to nonsentient machines), but a highly complicated bit of reasoning which depends on (A) the reification of universals[3] (e.g., "properties," "states," "events") ; and on (B) a sharp analytic-synthetic distinction.

I may be accused of advocating a "mechanistic" worldview in pressing the present analogy. If this means that I am supposed to hold that machines think,[4] on the one hand, or that human beings are machines, on the other, the charge is false. If there is some version of mechanism sophisticated enough to avoid these errors, very likely the considerations in this paper support it.[5]

1. TURING MACHINES

The present paper will require the notion of a *Turing machine*[6] which will now be explained.

Briefly, a Turing machine is a device with a finite number of internal configurations, each of which involves the machine's being in one of a finite number of *states*,[7] and the machine's scanning a tape on which certain symbols appear.

The machine's tape is divided into separate squares, thus:

on each of which a symbol (from a fixed finite alphabet) may be printed. Also the machine has a "scanner" which "scans" one square of the tape

---

[3] This point was made in Willard Van Orman Quine, "The Scope and Language of Science," *British Journal for the Philosophy of Science*, Vol. VIII (1957).

[4] Cf. Paul Ziff, "The Feelings of Robots" and J. J. C. Smart, "Professor Ziff on Robots" (below, pp. 98ff.) Ziff has informed me that by a "robot" he did not have in mind a "learning machine" of the kind envisaged by Smart, and he would agree that the considerations brought forward in his paper would not necessarily apply to such a machine (if it can properly be classed as a "machine" at all). On the question of whether "this machine thinks (feels, etc.)" is *deviant* or not, it is necessary to keep in mind both the point raised by Ziff (that the important question is not whether or not the utterance is deviant, but whether or not it is deviant for nontrivial reasons), and also the "diachronic-synchronic" distinction discussed in Sec. 5 below.

[5] In particular, I am sympathetic with the general standpoint taken by Smart in "Incompatible Colors," *Philosophical Studies*, Vol. X (1959), 39ff. and "Sensations and Brain Processes," *Philosophical Review*, Vol. LXVIII (1959), 141ff. However, see the linguistic considerations in Sec. 5.

[6] For further details, cf. Martin Davis, *Computability and Unsolvability* (New York: McGraw-Hill Book Company, Inc., 1958) and Stephen Cole Kleene, *Introduction to Metamathematics* (Princeton: D. Van Nostrand Co., Inc., 1952).

[7] This terminology is taken from Kleene, *op. cit.*, and differs from that of Davis and Turing.

at a time. Finally, the machine has a *printing mechanism* which may
(A) *erase* the symbol which appears on the square being scanned, and
(B) print some other symbol (from the machine's alphabet) on that
square.

Any Turing machine is completely described by a *machine table,*
which is constructed as follows: the rows of the table correspond to
letters of the alphabet (including the "null" letter, i.e., blank space),
while the columns correspond to states A,B,C, etc. In each square there
appears an "instruction," e.g., "s_5L A," "s_7C B," "s_3R C." These instructions are read as follows: "s_5L A" means "print the symbol s_5 on
the square you are now scanning (after erasing whatever symbol it
now contains), and proceed to scan the square immediately to the left of
the one you have just been scanning; also, shift into state A." The other
instructions are similarly interpreted ("R" means "scan the square
immediately to the *right,*" while "C" means "center," i.e., continue
scanning the *same* square). The following is a sample machine table:

		A	B	C	D
(s_1)	1	s_1RA	s_1LB	s_3LD	s_1CD
(s_2)	+	s_1LB	s_2CD	s_2LD	s_2CD
(s_3)	blank space	s_3CD	s_3RC	s_3LD	s_3CD

The machine described by this table is intended to function as follows:
the machine is started in state A. On the tape there appears a "sum"
(in unary notation) to be "worked out," e.g., "11 + 111."

The machine is initially scanning the first "1." The machine proceeds
to "work out" the sum (essentially by replacing the plus sign by a 1,
and then going back and erasing the first 1). Thus if the "input" was
1111 + 11111 the machine would "print out" 111111111, and then go
into the "rest state" (state D).

A "machine table" *describes* a machine if the machine has internal
states corresponding to the columns of the table, and if it "obeys" the
instructions in the table in the following sense: when it is scanning a
square on which a symbol s_1 appears and it is in, say, state B, that it
carries out the "instruction" in the appropriate row and column of the
table (in this case, column B and row s_1). Any machine that is described
by a machine table of the sort just exemplified is a Turing machine.

The notion of a Turing machine is also subject to generalization[8]

---

[8] This generalization is made in Davis, *op. cit.,* where it is employed in
defining relative recursiveness.

in various ways—for example, one may suppose that the machine has a second tape (an "input tape") on which additional information may be printed by an operator in the course of a computation. In the sequel we shall make use of this generalization (with electronic "sense organs" taking the place of the "operator").

It should be remarked that Turing machines are able in principle to do anything that any computing machine (of whichever kind) can do.[9]

It has sometimes been contended (e.g., by Nagel and Newman in their book *Gödel's Proof*) that "the theorem (i.e., Gödel's theorem) does indicate that the structure and power of the human mind are far more complex and subtle than any nonliving machine yet envisaged" (p. 10), and hence that a Turing machine cannot serve as a model for the human mind, but this is simply a mistake.

Let T be a Turing machine which "represents" me in the sense that T can prove just the mathematical statements I can prove. Then the argument (Nagel and Newman give no argument, but I assume they must have this one in mind) is that by using Gödel's technique I can discover a proposition that T cannot prove, and moreover *I* can prove this proposition. This refutes the assumption that T "represents" me, hence I am not a Turing machine. The fallacy is a misapplication of Gödel's theorem, pure and simple. Given an arbitrary machine T, all I can do is find a proposition U such that *I* can prove:

(3) If T is consistent, U is true,

where U is undecidable by T if T is in fact consistent. However, T can perfectly well prove (3) too! And the statement U, which T *cannot* prove (assuming consistency), I cannot prove either (unless I can prove that T is consistent, which is unlikely if T is very complicated)!

2. PRIVACY

Let us suppose that a Turing machine T is constructed to do the following. A number, say "3000," is printed on T's tape and T is started in T's "initial state." Thereupon T computes the 3000th (or whatever the given number was) digit in the decimal expansion of π, prints this digit on its tape, and goes into the "rest state," (i.e., turns itself off). Clearly the question "How does T 'ascertain' (or 'compute,' or 'work out') the 3000th digit in the decimal expansion of π?" is a

---

[9] This statement is a form of *Church's thesis* (that recursiveness equals effective computability).

sensible question. And the answer might well be a complicated one. In fact, an answer would probably involve three distinguishable constituents:

(i) A description of the sequence of states through which T passed in arriving at the answer, and of the appearance of the tape at each stage in the computation.

(ii) A description of the *rules* under which T operated (these are given by the "machine table" for T).

(iii) An explanation of the *rationale* of the entire procedure.

Now let us suppose that someone voices the following objection: "In order to perform the computation just described, T must pass through states A,B,C, etc. But how can T ascertain that it is in states A,B,C, etc.?"

It is clear that this is a silly objection. But what makes it silly? For one thing, the "logical description" (machine table) of the machine describes the states only in terms of their *relations* to each other and to what appears on the tape. The "physical realization" of the machine is immaterial, so long as there *are* distinct states A,B,C, etc., and they succeed each other as specified in the machine table. Thus one can answer a question such as "How does T ascertain that X?" (or "compute X," etc.) only in the sense of describing the *sequence of states* through which T must pass in ascertaining that X (computing X, etc.), the rules obeyed, etc. But there is no "sequence of states" through which T must pass to be in a single state!

Indeed, suppose there were—suppose T could not *be* in state A without first *ascertaining* that it was in state A (by first passing through a sequence of other states). Clearly a vicious regress would be involved. And one "breaks" the regress simply by noting that the machine, in ascertaining the 3000th digit in π, *passes through* its states—but it need not in any significant sense "ascertain" that it is passing through them.

Note the analogy to a fallacy in traditional epistemology: the fallacy of supposing that to know that p (where p is any proposition) one must first know that q_1, q_2, etc. (where q_1, q_2, etc., are appropriate *other* propositions). This leads either to an "infinite regress" or to the dubious move of inventing a special class of "protocol" propositions.

The resolution of the fallacy is also analogous to the machine case. Suppose that on the basis of sense experiences E_1, E_2, etc., I know that there is a chair in the room. It does not follow that I verbalized (or even *could* have verbalized) E_1, E_2, etc., nor that I remember E_1, E_2, etc., nor even that I "mentally classified" ("attended to," etc.) sense experiences E_1, E_2, etc., when I had them. In short, it is necessary to *have* sense experiences, but not to *know* (or even *notice*) what sense experiences one is having, in order to have certain kinds of knowledge.

Let us modify our case, however, by supposing that whenever the machine is in one particular state (say, "state A") it prints the words "I am in state A." Then someone might grant that the machine does not in general ascertain what state it is in, but might say in the case of state A (after the machine printed "I am in state A"): "The machine ascertained that it was in state A."

Let us study this case a little more closely. First of all, we want to suppose that when it is in state A the machine prints "I am in state A" without first passing through any other states. That is, in every row of the column of the table headed "state A" there appears the instruction: *print*[10] *"I am in State A."* Secondly, by way of comparison, let us consider a human being, Jones, who says "I am in pain" (or "Ouch!," or "Something hurts") whenever he is in pain. To make the comparison as close as possible, we will have to suppose that Jones' linguistic conditioning is such that he simply says "I am in pain" "without thinking," i.e., without passing through any introspectible mental states other than the pain itself. In Wittgenstein's terminology, Jones simply *evinces* his pain by saying "I am in pain"—he does not first reflect on it (or heed it, or note it, etc.) and then consciously describe it. (Note that this simple possibility of uttering the "proposition," "I am in pain" without first performing any mental "act of judgment" was overlooked by traditional epistemologists from Hume to Russell!) Now we may consider the parallel questions "Does the machine 'ascertain' that it is in state A?" and "Does Jones 'know' that he is in pain?" and their consequences.

Philosophers interested in semantical questions have, as one might expect, paid a good deal of attention to the verb "know." Traditionally, three elements have been distinguished: (1) "X knows that p" implies that p is *true* (we may call this the *truth* element); (2) "X knows that p" implies that X believes that p (philosophers have quarreled about the word, some contending that it should be 'X is *confident* that p,' or 'X is *in a position to assert* that p'; I shall call this element the *confidence* element); (3) "X knows that p" implies that X has evidence that p

---

[10] Here it is necessary to suppose that the entire sentence "I am in state A" counts as a single symbol in the machine's alphabet.

(here I think the word "evidence" is definitely wrong,[11] but it will not matter for present purposes; I shall call this the *evidential* element). Moreover, it is part of the meaning of the word "evidence" that nothing can be literally evidence for itself: if X is evidence for Y, then X and Y must be different things.

In view of such analyses, disputes have arisen over the propriety of saying (in cases like the one we are considering) "Jones knows that he is in pain." On the one hand, philosophers who take the common-sense view ("When I have a pain I *know* I have a pain") argue somewhat as follows: It would be clearly false to say Jones does *not* know he has a pain; but either Jones knows or he does not; hence, Jones knows he has a pain. Against these philosophers, one might argue as follows: "Jones does not know X" implies Jones is not in a position to assert that X; hence, it is certainly wrong to say "Jones does not know he has a pain." But the above use of the Law of the Excluded Middle was fallacious: words in English have *significance ranges,* and what is contended is that it is not semantically correct to say *either* "Jones knows that he has a pain" *or* "Jones does not know he has a pain" (although the former sentence is certainly less misleading than the latter, since *one* at least of the conditions involved in knowing is met—Jones is in a position to assert he has a pain. (In fact the *truth* and *confidence* elements are both present; it is the evidential element that occasions the difficulty.)

I do not wish to argue this question here;[12] the present concern is rather with the similarities between our two questions. For example, one might decide to accept (as "nondeviant," "logically in order," "nonselfcontradictory," etc.) the two statements:

(a) The machine ascertained that it was in state A,

(b) Jones knew that he had a pain,

or one might reject both. If one rejects (a) and (b), then one can find alternative formulations which are certainly semantically acceptable: e.g., [for (a)] "The machine was in state A, and this caused it to print: 'I am in state A'"; [for (b)] "Jones was in pain, and this caused him to say 'I am in pain'" (or, "Jones was in pain, and he evinced this by saying 'I am in pain'").

---

[11] For example, I know that the sun is 93 million miles from the earth, but I have no *evidence* that this is so. In fact, I do not even remember where I learned this.

[12] In fact, it would be impossible to decide whether "Jones knows he has a pain" is deviant or not without first reformulating the evidential condition so as to avoid the objection in note 11 (if it can be reformulated so as to save anything of the condition at all). However the discussion above will indicate, I believe, why one might *want* to find that this sentence is deviant.

On the other hand, if one accepts (a) and (b), then one must face the questions (a^1) *"How* did the machine ascertain that it was in state A?" and (b^1) *"How* did Jones know that he had a pain?"

And if one regards these questions as having answers at all, then they will be degenerate answers—e.g., "By being in state A" and "By having the pain."

At this point it is, I believe, very clear that the difficulty has in both cases the same cause. Namely, the difficulty is occasioned by the fact that the "verbal report" ("I am in state A," or "I am in pain") issues directly from the state it "reports": no "computation" or additional "evidence" is needed to arrive at the "answer." And the philosophic disagreements over "how to talk" are at bottom concerned with finding a terminology for describing cognitive processes in general that is not misleading in this particular case. [Note that the traditional epistemological answer to (b^1)—namely, "by introspection"—is false to the facts of this case, since it clearly implies the occurrence of a mental event (the "act" of introspection) distinct from the feeling of pain.]

Finally, let us suppose that the machine is equipped to "scan" its neighbor machine T^1. Then we can see that the question "How does T ascertain that T^1 is in state A?" may be a perfectly sensible question, as much so as "How does T ascertain that the 3000th digit of π is so-and-so?" In both cases the answer will involve describing a whole "program" (plus explaining the *rationale* of the program, if necessary). Moreover, it will be necessary to say something about the physical context linking T and T^1 (arrangement of sense organs, etc.), and not just to describe the internal states of T: this is so because T is now answering an *empirical* and not a mathematical question. In the same way "How did Sherlock Holmes know that Jones was in pain?" may be a perfectly sensible question, and may have quite a complicated answer.

3. "MENTAL" STATES AND "LOGICAL" STATES

Consider the two questions:
(1) How does Jones know he has a pain?
(2) How does Jones know he has a fever?

The first question is, as we saw in the preceding section, a somewhat peculiar one. The second question may be quite sensible. In fact, if Jones says "I have a pain" no one will retort "You are mistaken." (One *might* retort "You have made a slip of the tongue" or "You are lying," but not "You are *mistaken*.") On the other hand, if Jones says "I have a fever," the doctor who has just taken Jones' temperature may quite conceivably retort "You are mistaken." And the doctor need not mean that Jones made a linguistic error, or was lying, or confused.

It might be thought that, whereas the difference between statements about one's own state and statements about the state of others has an analogue in the case of machines, the difference, just touched upon, between statements about one's "mental" state and statements about one's "physical" state, in traditional parlance, does not have any analogue. But this is not so. Just what the analogue is will now be developed.

First of all, we have to go back to the notion of a Turing machine. When a Turing machine is described by means of a "machine table," it is described as something having a tape, a printing device, a "scanning" device (this may be no more than a point of the machine which at any given time is aligned with just one square of the tape), and a finite set (A,B,C, etc.) of "states." (In what follows, these will be referred to at times as *logical states* to distinguish them from certain other states to be introduced shortly.) Beyond this it is described only by giving the deterministic rules which determine the order in which the states succeed each other and what is printed when.

In particular, the "logical description" of a Turing machine does not include any specification of the *physical nature* of these "states"—or indeed, of the physical nature of the whole machine. (Shall it consist of electronic relays, of cardboard, of human clerks sitting at desks, or what?) In other words, a given "Turing machine" is an *abstract* machine which may be physically realized in an almost infinite number of different ways.

As soon as a Turing machine is physically realized, however, something interesting happens. Although the machine has from the logician's point of view only the states A,B,C, etc., it has from the engineer's point of view an almost infinite number of additional "states" (though not in the same sense of "state"—we shall call these *structural states*). For instance, if the machine consists of vacuum tubes, one of the things that may happen is that one of its vacuum tubes may fail—this puts the machine in what is from the physicist's if not the logician's point of view a different "state." Again, if the machine is a manually operated one built of cardboard, one of its possible "nonlogical" or "structural" states is obviously that its cardboard may buckle. And so on.

A physically realized Turing machine may have no way of ascertaining its own structural state, just as a human being may have no way of ascertaining the condition of his appendix at a given time. However, it is extremely convenient to give a machine electronic "sense organs" which enable it to scan itself and to detect minor malfunctions. These "sense organs" may be visualized as causing certain symbols to be printed on an "input tape" which the machine "examines" from time to time. (One minor difficulty is that the "report" of a sense organ might occupy a number of squares of tape, whereas the machine only "scans" one square at a time—however this is unimportant, since it is well known that the effect of "reading" any finite number of squares can be obtained using a program which only requires one square to be scanned at a time.)

(By way of a digression, let me remark that the first actually constructed digital computers did not have any devices of the kind just envisaged. On the other hand, they *did* have over 3000 vacuum tubes, some of which were failing at any given time! The need for "routines" for self-checking therefore quickly became evident.)[13]

A machine which is able to detect at least some of its own structural states is in a position very analogous to that of a human being, who can detect some but not all of the malfunctions of his own body, and with varying degrees of reliability. Thus, suppose the machine "prints out": "Vacuum tube 312 has failed." The question "How did the machine ascertain that vacuum tube 312 failed?" is a perfectly sensible question. And the answer may involve a reference to both the physical structure of the machine ("sense organs," etc.) and the "logical structure" (program for "reading" and "interpreting" the input tape).

If the machine prints: "Vacuum tube 312 has failed" when vacuum tube 312 is in fact functioning, the mistake may be due to a miscomputation (in the course of "reading" and "interpreting" the input tape) or to an incorrect signal from a sense organ. On the other hand, if the machine prints: "I am in state A," and it does this simply because its machine table contains the instruction: *Print: "I am in state A when in state A,"* then the question of a miscomputation cannot arise. Even if some accident causes the printing mechanism to print: "I am in state A" when the machine is *not* in state A, there was not a "miscomputation" (only, so to speak, a "verbal slip").

It is interesting to note that just as there are two possible descriptions

---

[13] Actually, it was not necessary to add any "sense organs"; existing computers check themselves by "performing crucial experiments with themselves" (i.e., carrying out certain test computations and comparing the results with the correct results which have been given).

of the behavior of a Turing machine—the engineer's structural blue-
print and the logician's "machine table"—so there are two possible descriptions of human psychology. The "behavioristic" approach (including
in this category theories which employ "hypothetical constructs," including "constructs" taken from physiology) aims at eventually providing a
complete physicalistic[14] description of human behavior, in terms which
link up with chemistry and physics. This corresponds to the engineer's
or physicist's description of a physically realized Turing machine. But
it would also be possible to seek a more abstract description of human
mental processes, in terms of "mental states" (physical realization, if
any, unspecified) and "impressions" (these play the role of symbols on
the machine's tapes)—a description which would specify the laws con-
trolling the order in which the states succeeded one another, and the
relation to verbalization (or, at any rate, verbalized thought). This
description, which would be the analogue of a "machine table," it was
in fact the program of classical psychology to provide! Classical psychology is often thought to have failed for *methodological* reasons; I would
suggest, in the light of this analogy, that it failed rather for empirical
reasons—the mental states and "impressions" of human beings do not
form a causally closed system to the extent to which the "configurations"
of a Turing machine do.

The analogy which has been presented between logical states of a
Turing machine and mental states of a human being, on the one hand,
and structural states of a Turing machine and physical states of a human
being, on the other, is one that I find very suggestive. In particular,
further exploration of this analogy may make it possible to further clarify
the notion of a "mental state" that we have been discussing. This "further exploration" has not yet been undertaken, at any rate by me, but
I should like to put down, for those who may be interested, a few of
the features that seem to distinguish logical and mental states respectively from structural and physical ones:

(1) The functional organization (problem solving, thinking) of the
human being or machine can be described in terms of the sequences of
mental or logical states respectively (and the accompanying verbaliza-
tions), without reference to the nature of the "physical realization" of
these states.

---

[14] In the sense of Paul Oppenheim and Hilary Putnam, "Unity of Science as
a Working Hypothesis," in *Concepts, Theories, and the Mind-Body Problem,*
H. Feigl, G. Maxwell, and M. Scriven, eds., Minnesota Studies in the Philosophy
of Science, Vol. II (Minneapolis: University of Minnesota Press, 1958); not in
the "epistemological" sense associated with Carnap's writings on "physicalism."

(2) The states seem intimately connected with *verbalization*.

(3) In the case of rational thought (or computing), the "program" which determines which states follow which, etc., is open to rational criticism.

4. MIND-BODY "IDENTITY"

The last area in which we have to compare human beings and machines involves the question of *identifying* mental states with the corresponding physical states (or logical states with the corresponding structural states). As indicated at the beginning of this paper, all of the arguments for and against such identification can perfectly well be discussed in terms of Turing machines.

For example, in the 1930's Wittgenstein used the following argument: If I observe an after-image, and observe at the same time my brain state (with the aid of a suitable instrument) I observe *two* things, not one. (Presumably this is an argument *against* identification.) But we can perfectly well imagine a "clever" Turing machine "reasoning" as follows: "When I print 'I am in state A,' I do not have to use my 'sense organs.' When I do use my 'sense organs,' and compare the occasions upon which I am in state A with the occasions upon which flip-flop 36 is on, I am comparing *two* things and not one." And I do not think that we would find the argument of this mechanical Wittgenstein very convincing!

By contrast, Russell once carried the "identity" view to the absurd extreme of maintaining that all we ever *see* is portions of our own brains. Analogously, a mechanical Russell might "argue" that "all I ever observe is my own vacuum tubes." Both "Russells" are wrong—the human being observes events in the outside world, and the process of "observation" involves events in his brain. But we are not therefore forced to say that he "really" observes his brain. Similarly, the machine T may "observe," say, cans of tomato soup (if the machine's job is sorting cans of soup), and the process of "observation" involves the functioning of vacuum tubes. But we are not forced to say that the machine "really" observes its own vacuum tubes.

But let us consider more serious arguments on this topic. At the beginning of this paper, I pointed out that the *synthetic* character of the statement (1) "I am in pain if, and only if, my C-fibers are stimulated" has been used as an argument for the view that the "properties" (or "events" or "states") "having C-fibers stimulated" and "being in

pain" cannot be the same. There are at least two reasons why this is not
a very good argument: (A) the "analytic-synthetic" distinction is not as
sharp as that, especially where scientific laws are concerned; and (B)
the criterion employed here for identifying "properties" (or "events"
or "states") is a very questionable one.

With respect to point (A): I have argued elsewhere[15] that fundamental scientific laws cannot be happily classified as either "analytic"
or "synthetic." Consider, for example, the kind of conceptual shift that
was involved in the transition from Euclidean to non-Euclidean geometry, or that would be involved if the law of the conservation of energy
were to be abandoned. It is a distortion to say that the laws of Euclidean
geometry (during their tenure of office) were "analytic," and that Einstein merely "changed the meaning of the words." Indeed, it was pre-
cisely because Einstein did *not* change the meaning of the words, because
he was really talking about shortest paths in the space in which we live
and move and have our being, that General Relativity seemed so incom-
prehensible when it was first proposed. To be told that one could come
back to the same place by moving in one direction on a straight line!
Adopting General Relativity was indeed adopting a whole new system
of concepts—but that is not to say "adopting a new system of verbal
labels."

But if it is a distortion to assimilate the revision of fundamental scientific laws to the adoption of new linguistic conventions, it is equally
a mistake to follow conventional philosophers of science, and assimilate
the conceptual change that Einstein inaugurated to the kind of change
that arises when we discover a black swan (whereas we had previously
assumed all swans to be white)! Fundamental laws are like principles
of pure mathematics (as Quine has emphasized), in that they cannot be
overthrown by isolated experiments: we can always hold on to the laws,
and explain the experiments in various more or less *ad hoc* ways. And—
in spite of the pejorative flavor of "ad hoc"—it is even *rational* to do
this, in the case of important scientific theories, *as long as no acceptable
alternative theory exists.* This is why it took a century of concept forma-
tion—and not just some experiments—to overthrow Euclidean geometry.
And similarly, this is why we cannot today describe *any* experiments
which would *by themselves* overthrow the law of the conservation of

---

[15] In Hilary Putnam, "The Analytic and the Synthetic," in *Scientific Explanation, Space, and Time,* H. Feigl and G. Maxwell, eds., Minnesota Studies
in the Philosophy of Science, Vol. III (Minneapolis: University of Minnesota
Press, 1962).

energy—although that law is not "analytic," and might be abandoned if a new Einstein were to suggest good *theoretical* reasons for abandoning it, plus supporting experiments.

As Hanson has put it,[16] our concepts have theories "built into" them —thus, to abandon a major scientific theory without providing an alternative would be to "let our concepts crumble." By contrast, although we *could* have held on to "all swans are white" in the face of conflicting evidence, there would have been no *point* in doing so—the concepts involved did not *rest* on the acceptance of this or some rival principle in the way that geometrical concepts rest on the acceptance, not necessarily of Euclidean geometry, but of *some* geometry.

I do not deny that *today* any newly-discovered "correlation" of the form: "One is in mental state ψ if, and only if, one is in brain state ϕ" would *at first* be a *mere* correlation, a pure "empirical generalization." But I maintain that the interesting case is the case that would arise if we had a worked out and theoretically elaborated *system* of such "correlations." In such a case, scientific talk would be very different. Scientists would begin to say: "It is impossible *in principle* to be in mental state ψ without being in brain state ϕ." And it could very well be that the "impossibility in principle" would amount to what Hanson rightly calls a *conceptual* [17] impossibility: scientists could not *conceive* (barring a new Einstein) of someone's being in mental state ψ without being in brain state ϕ. In particular, no experiment could *by itself* overthrow psychophysical laws which had acquired this kind of status.[18] Is it clear that in this kind of scientific situation it would not be correct to say that ϕ and ψ are the *same* state?

Moreover, the criteria for identifying "events" or "states" or "properties" are by no means so clear. An example of a law with the sort of status we have been discussing is the following: Light passes through an aperture if, and only if, electromagnetic radiation (of such-and-such wavelengths) passes through the aperture.

This law is quite clearly *not* an "analytic" statement. Yet it would be perfectly good scientific parlance to say that: (i) light passing through an aperture and (ii) electromagnetic radiation (of such-and-such wavelengths) passing through an aperture are two descriptions of the same event. (Indeed, in "ordinary language" not only are descriptions of the

[16] In Norwood Russell Hanson, *Patterns of Discovery* (London: Cambridge University Press, 1958).

[17] Cf. *Ibid.*

[18] Cf. the discussion of geometery in Putnam, *op. cit.*

same event not required to be equivalent: one may even speak of *incompatible* descriptions of the same event!)

It might be held, however, that *properties* (as opposed to events) cannot be described by different nonequivalent descriptions. Indeed, Frege, Lewis, and Carnap have *identified* properties and "meanings" (so that *by definition* if two expressions have different meanings then they "signify" different properties). This seems to me very dubious. But suppose it were correct. What would follow? One would have to admit that, e.g., being in pain and having C-fibers stimulated were different properties. But, in the language of the "theory-constructing" Turing machine described at the beginning of this paper, one would equally have to admit that "being in state A" and "having flip-flop 36 on" were different properties. Indeed the sentences (i) "I am in state A" and (ii) "Flip-flop 36 is on" are clearly nonsynonymous in the machine's language by any test (they have different syntactical properties and also different "conditions of utterance"—e.g., the machine has to use different "methods of verification"). Anyone who wishes, then, to argue on this basis for the existence of the soul will have to be prepared to hug the souls of Turing machines to his philosophic bosom!

5. A "LINGUISTIC" ARGUMENT

The last argument I shall consider on the subject of mind-body identity is a widely used "linguistic" argument—it was, for example, used by Max Black against Herbert Feigl at the Conference which inspired this volume. Consider the sentence:

(1) Pain *is identical with* stimulation of C-fibers.

The sentence is deviant (so the argument runs, though not in this terminology): there is no statement that it could be used to make in a normal context. Therefore, if a philosopher advances it as a thesis he must be giving the words a new meaning, rather than expressing any sort of discovery. For example (Max Black argued) one might begin to say "I have stimulated C-fibers" instead of "I have a pain," etc. But then one would *merely* be giving the expression "has stimulated C-fibers" the new meaning "is in pain." The contention is that as long as the words keep their present meanings, (1) is unintelligible.

I agree that the sentence (1) is a "deviant" sentence in present-day English. I do *not* agree that (1) can never become a normal, nondeviant sentence unless the words change their present meanings.

The point, in a nutshell, is that what is "deviant" depends very much upon context, including the state of our knowledge, and with the development of new scientific theories it is constantly occurring that sentences that did not previously "have a use," that were previously "deviant," acquire a use—not because the words acquire *new* meanings, but because the old meanings, as fixed by the core of stock uses, *determine* a new use given the new context.

There is nothing wrong with trying to bring linguistic theory to bear on this issue, but one must have a sufficiently sophisticated linguistic theory to bring to bear. The real question is not a question on *synchronic* linguistics but one on *diachronic*[19] linguistics, not "Is (1) *now* a deviant sentence?," but "If a change in scientific knowledge (e.g., the development of an integrated network of psychophysical laws of high "priority" in our over-all scientific world view) were to lead to (1)'s becoming a *non*deviant sentence, would a change in the meaning of a word necessarily have taken place?"—and this is not so simple a question.

Although this is not the time or the place to attempt the job of elaborating a semantical theory,[20] I should like to risk a few remarks on this question.

In the first place, it is easy to show that the mere uttering of a sentence which no one has ever uttered before does not necessarily constitute the introduction of a "new use." If I say "There is a purple Gila monster on this desk," I am very likely uttering a sentence that no English speaker has uttered before me: but I am not in any way changing the meaning of any word.

In the second place, even if a sentence which was formerly deviant begins to acquire a standard use, no change in the *meaning* of any word need have taken place. Thus the sentence "I am a thousand miles away from you," or its translation into ancient Greek, was undoubtedly a deviant sentence prior to the invention of *writing,* but acquired (was not "given," but *acquired*) a normal use with the invention of writing and the ensuing possibility of long-distance interpersonal address.

Note the reasons that we would not say that any word (e.g., "I," "you," "thousand") in this sentence changed its meaning: (A) the new

[19] Diachronic linguistics studies the language as it changes through time; synchronic linguistics seeks only to describe the language at one particular time.
[20] For a detailed discussion, cf. Ziff, *Semantic Analysis, op. cit.* I am extremely indebted to Ziff, both for making this work available to me and for personal communications on these matters. Section 5 of the present paper represents partly Ziff's influence (especially the use of the "synchronic-diachronic" distinction), and partly the application of some of the ideas of Putnam, *op. cit.* to the present topic.

use was not *arbitrary,* was not the product of *stipulation,* but represented an automatic projection[21] from the existing stock uses of the
several words making up the sentence, given the new context; (B) the
meaning of a sentence is in general a function of the meanings of the
individual words making it up (in fact this principle underlies the whole
notion of word meaning—thus, if we said that the *sentence* had changed
its meaning, we should have to face the question *"Which word* changed
its meaning?" But this would pretty clearly be an embarrassing question
in this case.

The case just described was one in which the new context was the
product of new technology, but new theoretical knowledge may have a
similar impact on the language. (For example, "he went all the way
around the world" would be a deviant sentence in a culture which did
not know that the earth was round!) A case of this kind was discussed
by Malcolm: We are beginning to have the means available for telling,
on the basis of various physiological indicators (electroencephalograms,
eye movements during sleep, blood pressure disturbances, etc.), when
dreams begin and end. The sentence "He is halfway through his dream"
may, therefore, someday acquire a standard use. Malcolm's comment
on this was that the words would in that case have been *given* a use.
Malcolm is clearly mistaken, I believe; this case, in which a sentence
acquires a use *because* of what the words mean is poles apart from the
case in which words are literally *given* a use (i.e., in which meanings
are stipulated for expressions). The "realistic" account of this case is,
I think, obviously correct: the sentence did not previously have a use
because we had no way of telling when dreams start and stop. Now
we are beginning to have ways of telling, and so we are beginning to
find occasions upon which it is natural to employ this sentence. (Note
that in Malcolm's account there is no explanation of the fact that we
give *this* sentence *this* use.)

Now, someone may grant that change in meaning should not be confused with change in distribution,[22] and that scientific and technological
advances frequently produce changes in the latter that are not properly
regarded as changes in the former. But one might argue that whereas
one could have envisaged beforehand the circumstances under which the
sentence "He went all the way around the world" would become nondeviant, one cannot now envisage any circumstances under which[23]

---

[21] The term is taken from Ziff, *Semantic Analysis, op. cit.*

[22] The *distribution* of a word = the set of sentences in which it occurs.

[23] Here "Mental state ψ is identical with brain state ϕ" is used as a surrogate
for such sentences as "Pain is identical with stimulation of C-fibers."

"mental state ψ is identical with brain state ϕ" would be nondeviant. But this is not a very good objection. In the first place, it might very well have been impossible for primitive people to envisage a spherical earth (the people on the "underside" would obviously fall off). Even forty years ago, it might have been difficult if not impossible to envisage circumstances under which "he is halfway through his dream" would be nondeviant. And in the second place, I believe that one *can* describe in general terms circumstances under which "mental state ψ is identical with brain state ϕ" would become nondeviant.

In order to do this, it is necessary to talk about one important kind of "is"—the *"is" of theoretical identification.* The use of "is" in question is exemplified in the following sentences:

(2) Light is electromagnetic radiation (of such-and-such wavelengths).

(3) Water is H_2O.

What was involved in the scientific acceptance of, for instance, (2) was very roughly this: prior to the identification there were two distinct bodies of theory—optical theory (whose character Toulmin has very well described in his book on philosophy of science), and electromagnetic theory (as represented by Maxwell's equations). The decision to *define* light as "electromagnetic radiation of such-and-such wavelengths" was scientifically justified by the following sorts of considerations (as has often been pointed out):

(1) It made possible the *derivation* of the laws of optics (up to first approximation) from more "basic" physical laws. Thus, even if it had accomplished nothing else, this theoretical identification would have been a move toward simplifying the structure of scientific laws.

(2) It made possible the derivation of *new* predictions in the "reduced" discipline (i.e., optics). In particular, it was now possible to predict that in certain cases the laws of geometrical optics would *not* hold. (Cf. Duhem's famous comments on the reduction of Kepler's laws to Newton's.)

Now let us try to envisage the circumstances under which a theoretical identification of mental states with physiological states might be in accordance with good scientific procedure. In general terms, what is necessary is that we should have not *mere* "correlates" for subjective states, but something much more elaborate—e.g., that we should know of physical states (say microstates of the central processes) on the basis of which we could not merely *predict* human behavior, but causally explain it.

In order to avoid "category mistakes," it is necessary to restrict this notion, "explain human behavior," very carefully. Suppose a man says "I feel bad." His behavior, described in one set of categories, is: "stating that he feels bad." And the explanation may be "He said that he felt bad because he was hungry and had a headache." I do not wish to suggest that the event "Jones *stating* that he feels bad" can be explained in terms of the laws of *physics*. But there is *another* event which is very relevant, namely "Jones' body producing such-and-such sound waves." From one point of view this is a "different event" from Jones' stating that he feels bad. But (to adapt a remark of Hanson's) there would be no point in remarking that these are different events if there were not a sense in which they were the *same* event. And it is the sense in which these are the "same event" and not the sense in which these are "different events" that is relevant here.

In fine, all I mean when I speak of "causally explaining human behavior" is: causally explaining certain physical events (notions of bodies, productions of sound waves, etc.) which are in the sense just referred to the "same" as the events which make up human behavior. And no amount of "Ryle-ism" can succeed in arguing away what is obviously a possibility: that physical science might succeed in doing this much.

If this much were a reality, then theoretically identifying "mental states" with their "correlates" would have the following two advantages:

(1) It would be possible (again up to "first approximation") to derive from physical theory the classical laws (or low-level generalizations) of common-sense "mentalistic" psychology, such as: "People tend to avoid things with which they have had painful experiences."

(2) It would be possible to predict the cases (and they are legion) in which common-sense "mentalistic" psychology fails.

Advantage (2) could, of course, be obtained without "identification" (by using correlation laws). But advantage (2) could equally have been obtained in the case of optics without identification (by assuming that light *accompanies* electromagnetic radiation, but is not *identical* with it). But the *combined* effect of eliminating certain laws altogether (in favor of theoretical definitions) *and* increasing the explanatory power of the theory could not be obtained in any other way in either case. The point worth noticing is that *every* argument for *and against* identification would apply equally in the mind-body case and in the light-electromagnetism case. (Even the "ordinary language" argument could have been advanced against the identification of light with electromagnetic radiation.)

Two small points: (i) When I call "light is electromagnetic radiation (of such-and-such wavelengths)" a definition, I do not mean that the statement is "analytic." But then "definitions," *properly so called,* in theoretical science virtually *never* are analytic.[24] (Quine remarked once that he could think of at least nine good senses of "definition," none of which had anything to do with analyticity.) Of course a philosopher might then object to the whole *rationale* of theoretical identification on the ground that it is no gain to eliminate "laws" in favor of "definitions" if both are *synthetic* statements. The fact that the scientist does not feel at all the same way is another illustration of how unhelpful it is to look at science from the standpoint of the question "Analytic or synthetic?" (ii) Accepting a theoretical identification, e.g., "Pain *is* stimulation of C-fibers," does not commit one to *interchanging* the terms "pain" and "stimulation of C-fibers" in idiomatic talk, as Black suggested. For instance, the identification of "water" with "H_2O" is by now a very well-known one, but no one says "Bring me a glass of H_2O," except as a joke.

I believe that the account just presented is able (a) to explain the fact that sentences such as "Mental state ψ is identical with brain state ϕ" are deviant in present-day English, while (b) making it clear how these same sentences might become *non*deviant given a suitable increase in our scientific insight into the physical nature and causes of human behavior. The sentences in question cannot today be used to express a theoretical identification, because no such identification has been made. The act of theoretical identification is not an act that can be performed "at will"; there are *preconditions* for its performance, as there are for many acts, and these preconditions are not satisfied today. On the other hand, if the sort of scientific theory described above should materialize, then the preconditions for theoretical identification would be met, as they were met in the light-electromagnetism case, and sentences of the type in question would then *automatically* require a use—namely, to express the appropriate theoretical identifications. Once again, what makes this way of *acquiring* a use different from being *given* a use (and from "change of meaning" properly so called) is that the "new use" is an automatic *projection* from existing uses, and does not involve arbitrary stipulation (except insofar as some element of "stipulation" may be present in the acceptance of *any* scientific hypothesis, including "The earth is round").

So far we have considered only sentences of the form[25] "mental state

---

[24] This is argued in Putnam, *op. cit.*

[25] By sentences of this *form* I do not literally mean *substitution instances* of "mental state ψ is identical with brain state ϕ." Cf. note 23.

ψ is identical with brain state ϕ." But what of the sentence:
(3) Mental states are microstates of the brain?

This sentence does not, so to speak, "give" any *particular* theoretical identification: it only says that unspecified theoretical identifications are possible. This is the sort of assertion that Feigl might make. And Black[26] might reply that in uttering (3) Feigl had uttered an odd set of words (i.e., a deviant sentence). It is possible that Black is right. Perhaps (3) is deviant in present-day English. But it is also possible that our descendants in two or three hundred years will feel that Feigl was making perfectly good sense, and that the linguistic objections to (3) were quite silly. And they too may be right.

6. MACHINE LINGUISTICS

Let us consider the linguistic question that we have just discussed from the standpoint of the analogy between man and Turing machine that we have been presenting in this paper. It will be seen that our Turing machine will probably not be able, if it lacks suitable "sense organs," to construct a correct theory of its own constitution. On the other hand "I am in state A" will be a sentence with a definite pattern of occurrence in the machine's "language." If the machine's "language" is sufficiently complex, it may be possible to analyze it syntactically in terms of a finite set of basic building blocks (morphemes) and rules for constructing a potentially infinite set of "sentences" from these. In particular, it will be possible to distinguish *grammatical* [27] from *ungrammatical sentences* in the machine's "language." Similarly, it may be possible to associate regularities with sentence occurrences (or, "describe sentence uses," in the Oxford jargon), and to assign "meanings" to the finite set of morphemes and the finite set of forms of composition, in such a way that the "uses" of the various sentences can be effectively projected from the meanings of the individual morphemes and forms of composition. In this case, one could distinguish not only "grammatical" and "ungrammatical" sentences in the "machine language," but also "deviant" and "nondeviant" ones.

Chisholm would insist that it is improper to speak of machines as employing a language, and I agree. This is the reason for my occasionally

---

[26] I have, with hesitation, ascribed this position to Black on the basis of his remarks at the conference. But, of course, I realize that he cannot justly be held responsible for remarks made on the spur of the moment.

[27] This term is used in the sense of (3), not in the traditional sense.

enclosing the words "language," "meaning," etc., in "raised-eyebrow" quotes—to emphasize, where necessary, that these words are being used in an extended sense. On the other hand, it is important to recognize that machine performances may be wholly *analogous* to language, so much so that the whole of linguistic theory can be applied to them. If the reader wishes to check this, he may go through a work like Chomsky's *Syntactic Structures* carefully, and note that *at no place is the assumption employed that the corpus of utterances studied by the linguist was produced by a conscious organism.* Then he may turn to such pioneer work in empirical semantics as Ziff's *Semantic Analysis* and observe that the same thing holds true for *semantical* theory.

Two further remarks in this connection: (i) Since I am contending that the mind-body problem is *strictly analogous* to the problem of the relation between structural and logical states, not that the two problems are *identical,* a suitable *analogy* between machine "language" and human language is all that is needed here. (ii) Chisholm might contend that a "behavioristic" semantics of the kind attempted by Ziff (i.e., one that does not take "intentionality" as a primitive notion) is impossible. But even if this were true, it would not be relevant. For if *any* semantical theory can fit human language, it has to be shown why a completely *analogous* theory would not fit the language of a suitable machine. For instance, if "intentionality" plays a role as a primitive notion in a *scientific* explanation of human language, then a theoretical construct with similar *formal* relations to the corresponding "observables" will have the *same* explanatory power in the case of machine "language."

Of course, the objection to "behavioristic" linguistics might *really* be an objection to all attempts at *scientific* linguistics. But this possibility I feel justified in dismissing.

Now suppose we equip our "theory-constructing" Turing machine with "sense organs" so that it can obtain the empirical data necessary for the construction of a theory of its own nature.

Then it may introduce into its "theoretical language" noun phrases that can be "translated" by the English expression "flip-flop 36," and sentences that can be translated by "Flip-flop 36 is on." These expressions will have a meaning and use quite distinct from the meaning and use of "I am in state A" in the machine language.

If any "linguistic" argument really shows that the sentence "Pain is identical with stimulation of C-fibers" is deviant, in English, the same argument must show that "State A is identical with flip-flop 36 being on" is deviant in the machine language. If any argument shows that "Pain is identical with stimulation of C-fibers" could not become nondeviant (viewing English now *dia*chronically) unless the words first altered their meanings, the same argument, applied to the "diachronic linguistics of machine language," would show that the sentence "State A is identical with flip-flop 36 being on" could not become nondeviant in machine language unless the words first changed their meanings. In short, every philosophic argument that has ever been employed in connection with the mind-body problem, from the oldest and most naïve (e.g., "states of consciousness can just be *seen* to be different from physical states") to the most sophisticated, has its exact counterpart in the case of the "problem" of logical states and structural states in Turing machines.

7. CONCLUSION

The moral, I believe, is quite clear: it is no longer possible to believe that the mind-body problem is a genuine theoretical problem, or that a "solution" to it would shed the slightest light on the world in which we live. For it is quite clear that no grown man in his right mind would take the problem of the "identity" or "nonidentity" of logical and structural states in a machine at all seriously—not because the answer is obvious, but because it is obviously of no importance *what* the answer is. But if the so-called "mind-body problem" is nothing but a different realization of the same set of logical and linguistic issues, then it must be just as empty and just as verbal.

It is often an important insight that two problems with distinct subject matter are the same in all their logical and methodological aspects. In this case, the insight carries in its train the realization that any conclusion that might be reached in the case of the mind-body problem would have to be reached, *and for the same reasons,* in the Turing machine case. But if it is clear (as it obviously is) that, for example, the conclusion that the logical states of Turing machines are hopelessly different from their structural states, even if correct, could represent only a purely *verbal* discovery, then the same conclusion *reached by the same arguments* in the human case must likewise represent a purely verbal discovery. To put it differently, if the mind-body problem is identified with any problem of more than purely conceptual interest (e.g., with the question of whether or not human beings have "souls"), then *either* it must be that (a) no argument *ever* used by a philosopher sheds the *slightest* light on it (and this independently of the way the argument tends), or (b) that some philosophic argument for mechanism is correct, or (c) that some dualistic argument does show that *both* human beings *and* Turing machines have souls! I leave it to the reader to decide which of the three alternatives is at all plausible.

THE FEELINGS

OF ROBOTS

PAUL ZIFF

Could a robot have feelings? Some say of course.[1] Some say of course not.[2]

1. I want the right sort of robots. They must be automata and without doubt machines.

I shall assume that they are essentially computing machines, having microelements and whatever micromechanisms may be necessary for the functioning of these engineering wonders. Furthermore, I shall assume that they are powered by microsolar batteries: instead of having lunch they will have light.

And if it is clear that our robots are without doubt machines then in all other respects they may be as much like men as you like. They may

"*The Feelings of Robots*," Analysis, *Vol. XIX, No. 3 (1959). Reprinted by permission of the editior of* Analysis.
[1] Cf. D. M. MacKay, "The Epistemological Problem for Automata," in *Automata Studies* (Princeton: Princeton University Press, 1956), pp. 235ff.
[2] Cf. M. Scriven, "The Mechanical Concept of Mind" (see above, pp. 31ff.).

be the size of men. When clothed and masked they may be virtually indistinguishable from men in practically all respects: in appearance, in movement, in the utterances they utter, and so forth. Thus except for the masks any ordinary man would take them to be ordinary men. Not suspecting they were robots nothing about them would make him suspect.

But unmasked the robots are to be seen in all their metallic lustre. What is in question here is not whether we can blur the line between a man and a machine and so attribute feelings to the machine. The question is whether we can attribute feelings to the machine and so blur the line between a man and a machine.

2. Could robots have feelings? Could they, say, feel tired, or bored?

Ex hypothesi robots are mechanisms, not organisms, not living creatures. There could be a broken-down robot but not a dead one. Only living creatures can literally have feelings.

If I say "She feels tired" one can generally infer that what is in question is (or was or will be in the case of talk about spirits)[3] a living creature. More generally, the linguistic environment ". . . feels tired" is generally open only to expressions that refer to living creatures. Suppose you say "The robot feels tired." The phrase "the robot" refers to a mechanism. Then one can infer that what is in question is not a living creature. But from the utterance of the predicative expression ". . . feels tired" one can infer that what is in question is a living creature. So if you are speaking literally and you say "The robot feels tired" you imply a contradiction. Consequently one cannot literally predicate ". . . feels tired" of "the robot."

Or again: no robot will ever do everything a man can. And it doesn't matter how robots may be constructed or how complex and varied their movements and operations may be. Robots may calculate but they will not literally reason. Perhaps they will take things but they will not literally borrow them. They may kill but not literally murder. They may voice apologies but they will not literally make any. These are actions that only persons can perform: *ex hypothesi* robots are not persons.

3. "A dead robot" is a metaphor but "a dead battery" is a dead metaphor: if there were a robot around it would put its metaphor to death.

What I don't want to imply I need not imply. An implication can be weakened. The sense of a word can be widened or narrowed or shifted. If one wishes to be understood then one mustn't go too far: that is all. Pointing to one among many paintings, I say "Now *that*

---

[3] I shall henceforth omit the qualification.

one is a *painting*." Do I mean the others are not? Of course not. Yet the stress on "that" is contrastive. So I say "The robot, that mechanism, not of course a living creature but a machine, it feels tired": you cannot infer that what is in question here is a living creature.

If I say of a person "He feels tired," do you think I am saying that he is a living creature and only that? If I say "The robot feels tired" I am not saying that what is in question is a living creature, but that doesn't mean that nothing is being said. If I say "The robot feels tired," the predicate ". . . feels tired" means whatever it usually means except that one cannot infer that what is in question is a living creature. That is the only difference.

And what has been said about "The robot feels tired" could be said equally well about "The robot is conscious," "The robot borrowed my cat," and so forth.

4. Could robots feel tired? Could a stone feel tired? Could the number 17 feel tired? It is clear that there is no reason to believe that 17 feels tired. But that doesn't prove anything. A man can feel tired and there may be nothing, there need be nothing at all, that shows it. And so with a robot or a stone or the number 17.

Even so, the number 17 could not feel tired. And I say this not because or not simply because there are no reasons to suppose that 17 does feel tired but because there are good reasons not to suppose that 17 feels tired and good reasons not to suppose that 17 ever feels anything at all. Consequently it is necessary to consider whether there are any reasons for supposing that robots feel tired and whether there are good reasons for not supposing that robots ever feel anything at all.

5. Knowing George and seeing the way he looks I say he feels tired. Knowing Josef and seeing the way he looks I don't say he feels tired. Yet if you don't know either of them then to you George and Josef may look alike.

In one sense they may look alike to me too, but not in another. For George but not Josef will look tired. If you ask me to point out the difference there may be nothing relevant, there need be nothing relevant, to point to. For the relevant difference may be like that between looking at an unframed picture and looking at it framed. Only the frame here is provided by what I know about them: you cannot see what I know.

(Speaking with the robots, one can say that the way things look to me, my present output, will not be the same as yours, the way things look to you, even though at present we may both receive the same input, the same stimuli, and this is because your mechanism was not in the same initial state as mine, owing either to a difference in structure or to a difference in previous inputs.)

If we say of a person that he feels tired, we generally do so not only on the basis of what we see then and there but on the basis of what we have seen elsewhere and on the basis of how what we have seen elsewhere ties in with what we see then and there. And this is only to say that in determining whether or not a person feels tired both observational and theoretic considerations are involved and, as everywhere, are inextricably interwoven.

6. Suppose you and I visit an actor at home. He is rehearsing the role of a grief-stricken man. He ignores our presence as a grief-stricken man might. His performance is impeccable. I know but you do not know that he is an actor and that he is rehearsing a role. You ask "Why is he so miserable?" and I reply "He isn't." "Surely," you say, "he is grief-stricken. Look at him! Show me what leads you to say otherwise!" and of course there may be nothing then and there to show.

So Turing[4] posed the question whether automata could think, be conscious, have feelings, etc., in the following naïve way: what test would an automaton fail to pass? MacKay[5] has pointed out that any test for mental or any other attributes to be satisfied by the observable activity of a human being can be passed by automata. And so one is invited to say what would be wrong with a robot's performance.

Nothing need be wrong with either the actor's or a robot's performance. What is wrong is that they are performances.

7. Suppose K is a robot. An ordinary man may see K and not knowing that K is a robot, the ordinary man may say "K feels tired." If I ask him what makes him think so, he may reply "K worked all day digging ditches. Anyway, just look at K: if he doesn't look tired, who does?"

So K looks tired to the ordinary man. That doesn't prove anything. If I know K is a robot, K may not look tired to me. It is not what I see but what I know. Or it is not what I see then and there but what I have seen elsewhere. Where? In a robot psychology laboratory.

8. If I say "The robot feels tired," the predicate ". . . feels tired" means whatever it usually means except that one cannot infer that what is in question is a living creature. That is the only difference.

---

[4] Cf. "Computing Machinery and Intelligence" (see above, pp. 4ff.).
[5] Cf. "Mentality in Machines," *Proceedings of the Aristotelian Society*, Supp. Vol. XXVI (1952), 61ff.

To speak of something living is to speak of an organism in an environment. The environment is that in which the behavior of the organism takes place. Death is the dissolution of the relation between an organism and its environment. In death I am pluralized, converted from one to many. I become my remains. I merge with my environment.

If we think of robots being put together, we can think of them being taken apart. So in our laboratory we have taken robots apart, we have changed and exchanged their parts, we have changed and exchanged their programs, we have started and stopped them, sometimes in one state, sometimes in another, we have taken away their memories, we have made them seem to remember things that were yet to come, and so on.

And what we find in our laboratory is this: no robot could sensibly be said to feel anything. Why not?

9. Because there are not psychological truths about robots but only about the human makers of robots. Because the way a robot acts (in a specified context) depends primarily on how we programed it to act. Because we can program a robot to act in any way we want it to act. Because a robot could be programed to act like a tired man when it lifted a feather and not when it lifted a ton. Because a robot couldn't mean what it said any more than a phonograph record could mean what it said. Because we could make a robot say anything we want it to say. Because coveting thy neighbor's robot wife would be like coveting his car and not like coveting his wife. Because robots are replaceable. Because robots have no individuality. Because one can duplicate all the parts and have two virtually identical machines. Because one can exchange all the parts and still have the same machines. Because one can exchange the programs of two machines having the same structure. Because. . . .

Because no robot would act tired. Because a robot could only act like a robot programed to act like a tired man. For suppose some robots are programed to act like a tired man after lifting a feather while some are so programed that they never act like a tired man. Shall we say "It is a queer thing but some robots feel tired almost at once while others never feel tired"? Or suppose some are programed to act like a tired man after lifting something blue but not something green. Shall we say "Some robots feel tired when they lift blue things but not when they lift green things"? And shall we conclude "Some robots find blue things heavier than green things"? Hard work makes a man feel tired: what will make a robot act like a tired man? Perhaps hard work, or light work, or no work, or anything at all. For it will depend on the whims of the man who makes it (though these whims may be modified by whatever quirks may appear in the robot's electronic nerve network, and there may be unwanted and unforeseen consequences of an ill-conceived program). Shall we say "There's no telling what will make a robot feel tired"? And if a robot acts like a tired man then what? Some robots may be programed to require a rest, others to require more work. Shall we say "This robot feels tired so put it back to work"?

What if all this were someday to be done with and to human beings? What if we were someday to break down the difference between a man and his environment? Then someday we would wake and find that we are robots. But we wouldn't wake to a mechanical paradise or even an automatic hell: for then it might not make sense to talk of human beings having feelings just as it now doesn't make sense to talk of robots having feelings.

A robot would behave like a robot.

PROFESSOR ZIFF

ON ROBOTS

J. J. C. SMART

Professor Ziff ("The Feelings of Robots") argues that robots could not have feelings. Only living things, he says, could have feelings, and robots could not be living things. Both his premise and his conclusion seem to me to be questionable, though in a brief note I can touch on some only of my reasons for thinking this.

(A) The notion of "living thing" as opposed to "robot" is unclear.

(1) Let us pretend that the *Genesis* story is literally true. Then Adam and Eve were robots. They were artifacts fashioned by God. If a conflation of ancient theology and modern biology may be allowed, we could even say that God gave Adam and Eve "programs," namely their sets of genes, probably DNA molecules which have the function of recording hereditary information.

"Professor Ziff on Robots," Analysis, *Vol. XIX, No. 5 (1959). Reprinted by permission of the author and the editor of* Analysis.

(2) Consider von Neumann's self-reproducing mechanism. (John von Neumann, "The General and Logical Theory of Automata," *Cerebral Mechanisms in Behaviour,* The Hixon Symposium, 1951, pp. 1-31.) In what sense would descendants of such a mechanism be any the less living creatures than descendants of Adam and Eve? We could even suppose small random alterations in that part of them which records their design. Such machines could evolve by natural selection and develop propensities and capacities which did not belong to the original machine.

(1) and (2) taken together show how unclear is the distinction between a (sufficiently complex) artifact and a living creature. I myself find this not in the least surprising, for I am inclined to accept the physicalist thesis that living creatures just are very complicated physico-chemical mechanisms.

(B) I cannot see why "this has feelings" entails "this is a living creature," if "this is a living creature" is taken to entail "this is not an artifact." None of the artifacts any of us have met in practice have been sufficiently complex to warrant the assertion that they have feelings. So we should in fact at present run into no trouble if we deduced "this is a living creature" if told "this has feelings." Nevertheless it need not be a logical entailment. Maybe in the future we shall find counterexamples.

(C) Suppose we made a robot so complex that it could learn new purposes and capacities in the way that a child can. (Compare Turing's child-machine, in "Computing Machinery and Intelligence." It might even become a philosopher, attending conferences, and developing just as human philosophers do. Why should we not say that it *meant* what it said? It would not be at all analogous to Ziff's machine with a phonograph record inside.

In short, therefore, I find Ziff's arguments unconvincing. I suspect that I may have misunderstood their purport, but I feel that Ziff could have made his intentions plainer.

ROBOTS INCORPORATED

NINIAN SMART

Paul Ziff, discussing robots (pp. 98-103), gives a number of reasons why it is not to be said that they feel tired and so on. I shall urge that his reasons would not persuade a determinist, except insofar as he is bringing out this point: that his robots do not feel because they do not have proper bodies. I shall then argue that this does not help much to see why certain artifacts do not feel. One does not, of course, need to be a determinist; but if one is not, and unless unrealistically one is going to compartmentalize human beings, the reasons why human beings feel tired and robots do not must go much deeper. I shall not deal with all Ziff's reasons, but will concentrate on certain of them to be found in Section 9 of his article, which I take to be crucial. Robots, he argues do not feel because:—

1. "The way a robot acts (in a specified context) depends primarily

"Robots Incorporated," Analysis, *Vol. XIX, No. 5 (1959). Reprinted by permission of the author and the editor of* Analysis.

on how we programed [1] it to act." For the sake of simplicity I introduce the notion of Nature to represent the sum of causes going towards
the creation of a human being considered as beginning with conception
or at any later time in his life. What is wrong, for the determinist, in
saying that the way a man acts, in a specified context, depends primarily
on how Nature programs him to act? Subtle programs, of course; much
subtler than computer programs, but the subtle cell circuits still determine the way I act, given a situation.

2. "We can program a robot to act in any way we want it to act."
Nature does not want things, so in a way the parallel does not hold.
But this is a side issue: for the status of an effect need not be affected
by the status of the cause. Is Ziff then bringing out our sense of power
over robots? Not quite, for we might gain what appears to be a similar
power over the animal kingdom through crafty breeding (give me a cat
that loves mice—but don't think you are giving me a cat that cannot
feel). No, the special sort of power is brought out as follows:

3. "Because a robot could be programed to act like a tired man when
it lifted a feather and not when it lifted a ton." The power is that the
same structure can be programed opposite ways, not that different robots
can be built that operate oppositely (we cannot breed a cat, perhaps,
that loves mice until we change its program). For the determinist, the
trouble is that Ziff's robot does not possess a proper body: it is not
fully incorporated. Nature gives the cat its program (or set of programs) with its body, and for a new program you need a new body.

4. "You can duplicate all the parts." Nature replaces all or most of
the parts every so often. And Nature produces identical twins. For that
matter Nature might produce centuplets—it is a dull but logically possible world where human beings roll out of the womb with the regularity
and indistinguishability of Cadillacs.

These examples seem to show that, for a determinist reading Ziff,
it is the body that counts. Ziff says at the outset that he wants the right
kind of robot—one which is essentially a computing machine.[2] And such
a one he contrasts with a living organism, which is separate from its
environment and where death is a merging into the environment.[3]
Briefly: his robot is where you have the same valves and different programs; the organism is where you have the same body and the same
program (or set of programs).

---

[1] In what follows, both Ziff and I use "program" in a rather wide sense.
[2] p. 98.
[3] p. 102.

Embodiment, then, comes essentially to this: a robot is embodied if and only if, in order to reprogram it, it is necessary both to dismantle it and to rebuild it in a different way. This is sufficient to accommodate Ziff's crucial point 3 above. But if Ziff can conceive of a robot which can go through the motions of being tired, you can also conceive of a more inefficient specimen which could not be programed to act tired when lifting a feather. But do we want to say that this one feels tired sometimes?

How then are we to pinpoint the difference between embodied robots which do not feel and those embodied beings which do? The only suggestion that springs readily to mind is that it has something to do with subtlety and complexity. Certain mechanical toys are embodied in the above sense, but they are crude. But the criteria of subtlety and complexity are too vague to be useful. And in any case we have a lurking feeling about ghosts. A Ziff robot does not feel because it is a machine in a ghost, not because there is no ghost in the machine. But to be told that robots do not feel because they do not have bodies, though it makes us pause to cogitate, leaves us unhappy too.

SELECTED

BIBLIOGRAPHY

I have included all bibliographical material which accompanied the articles in this anthology (together with place and date of original publication). I have also listed a number of other articles of interest, but I have not tried to assemble a complete list of books and articles on "Minds and Machines"—partly because of limitations of space, but more importantly because admirable comprehensive bibliographies are' already in existence: see Armer, Minsky (especially his ". . . Bibliography to the Literature on Artificial Intelligence"), or Simmons and Simmons (all listed below).

Anisimov, S. F., *Man and Machine* (*Philosophical Problems of Cybernetics*), Report No. JPRS 1990-N. Washington, D.C.: Joint Publications Research Service, 1959.

Armer, Paul, *Attitudes Toward Intelligent Machines*. Santa Monica, Cal.: The RAND Corporation, 1962.

Ashby, W. R., "Can a Mechanical Chess Player Outplay Its Designer?" *British Journal for the Philosophy of Science,* Vol. III (1952), 44-47.

———, *Design for a Brain*. New York: John Wiley & Sons, Inc., 1954.

Blake, D. V. and A. M. Uttley, eds., *Proceedings of a Symposium on Mechanization of Thought Processes,* 2 vols. London: Her Majesty's Stationery Office, 1959.

Burks, Arthur W., "Computation, Behavior, and Structure in Fixed and Growing Automata," *Behavioral Science,* Vol. VI, No. 1 (1961), 5-22.

Butler, Samuel, *Erewhon.* Chaps. 23-25.

Carnap, Rudolf, "The Interpretation of Physics," in *Readings in the Philosophy of Science,* H. Feigl and M. Brodbeck, eds., pp. 309-318. New York: Appleton-Century-Crofts, Inc., 1953.

————, "The Methodological Character of Theoretical Concepts," in *Foundations of Science and the Concepts of Psychology and Psychoanalysis,* H. Feigl and M. Scriven, eds., Minnesota Studies in the Philosophy of Science, Vol. I, pp. 38-76. Minneapolis: University of Minnesota Press, 1956.

Chappell, V. C., ed., *The Philosophy of Mind.* Englewood Cliffs, N.J.: Prentice-Hall, Inc., 1962.

Chomsky, Noam, *Syntactic Structures.* The Hague: Mouton & Co., 1957.

Church, Alonzo, *Introduction to Mathematical Logic.* Princeton: Princeton University Press, 1956.

————, "An Unsolvable Problem of Elementary Number Theory," *American Journal of Mathematics,* Vol. LVIII (1936), 345-363.

Cohen, Jonathan, "Can There Be Artificial Minds?" *Analysis,* Vol. XVI (1955), 36-41.

Copi, I. M., C. C. Elgot, and J. B. Wright, "Realization of Events by Logical Nets," *Journal for the Association of Computing Machinery,* Vol. V (1958), 181-196.

Danto, Arthur C., "On Consciousness in Machines," in *Dimensions of Mind,* Sidney Hook, ed., pp. 180-187. New York: New York University Press, 1960.

Davis, Martin, *Computability and Unsolvability.* New York: McGraw-Hill Book Company, Inc., 1958.

Friedberg, R. M., "A Learning Machine," Part I, *IBM Journal of Research and Development,* Vol. II (1958), 2-13.

Gelernter, H. L., "Realization of a Geometry-Proving Machine," *Proceedings of the International Conference on Information Processing.* Paris: UNESCO House, 1959.

George, F. H., "Logic and Behavior," *Science News,* Vol. XLV (1957), 46-60.

Gödel, Kurt, "Über Formal Unentscheidbare Sätze der Principia Mathematica und verwandter Systeme," Part I, *Monatshefte für Mathematik und Physik,* Vol. XXXVIII (1931), 173-189.

Haldane, J. B. S., "The Mechanical Chess-Player," *British Journal for the Philosophy of Science,* Vol. III (1952), 189-191.

Hanson, Norwood Russell, *Patterns of Discovery.* London: Cambridge University Press, 1958.

Hartree, D. R., *Calculating Instruments and Machines.* Urbana: University of Illinois Press, 1949.

Jefferson, G., "The Mind of Mechanical Man," Lister Oration for 1949, *British Medical Journal,* Vol. I (1949), 1105-1121.

Kleene, Stephen Cole, "General Recursive Functions of Natural Numbers," *American Journal of Mathematics,* Vol. LVII (1935), 153-173, 219-244.

——, *Introduction to Metamathematics.* Princeton: D. Van Nostrand Co., Inc., 1952.

Lacey, A. R., "Men and Robots," *Philosophical Quarterly,* Vol. X (1960), 61-72.

Lovelace, Mary Caroline, Countess of, *Scientific Memoirs,* R. Taylor, ed., Vol. III (1842), pp. 691-731.

Lucas, J. R., "The Lesbian Rule," *Philosophy,* Vol. XXX (1955), 195-213.

——, "Minds, Machines, and Gödel," *Philosophy,* Vol. XXXVI (1961), 112-127.

——, "On Not Worshipping Facts," *Philosophical Quarterly,* Vol. VIII (1958), 144-156.

MacKay, D. M., "The Epistemological Problem for Automata," *Automata Studies,* pp. 235-251. Princeton: Princeton University Press, 1956.

——, "Mentality in Machines," *Proceedings of the Aristotelian Society,* Supp. Vol. XXVI (1952), 61-86.

——, "Mind-Like Behaviour in Artifacts," *British Journal for the Philosophy of Science,* Vol. II, No. 6 (1951), 110.

——, "Operational Aspects of Intellect," *Proceedings of the Symposium on Mechanization of Thought Processes,* D. V. Blake and A. M. Uttley, eds. London: Her Majesty's Stationery Office, 1959.

McCulloch, W. S., "The Brain as a Computing Machine," *Electrical Engineering,* Vol. LXVIII (1949), 492-497.

—— and J. E. Pfeiffer, "Of Digital Computers Called Brains," *Scientific Monthly,* Vol. LXIX (1949), 368-376.

Mays, W., "The Hypothesis of Cybernetics," *British Journal for the Philosophy of Science,* Vol. II, No. 7 (1951), 249-250.

Minsky, Marvin L., "Heuristic Aspects of the Artificial Intelligence Problem," Group Report 34-55; Massachusetts Institute of Technology, Lincoln Laboratory, Lexington, December 1956.

———, "A Selected Descriptor-Indexed Bibliography to the Literature on Artificial Intelligence," *IRE Transactions on Human Factors in Electronics* (1961), 39-55.

———, "Steps Toward Artificial Intelligence," *Proceedings of the IRE,* Vol. XLIX, No. 1 (1961), 8-30.

Nagel, Ernest and J. R. Newman, *Gödel's Proof.* New York: New York University Press, 1958.

Newell, A., J. C. Shaw, and H. A. Simon, "Elements of a Theory of Human Problem Solving," *Psychological Review,* Vol. LXV (1958), 151-166.

Newell, A. and H. A. Simon, *The Simulation of Human Thought,* Report No. P-1734. Santa Monica, Cal.: The RAND Corporation, 1959.

Oppenheim, Paul and Hilary Putnam, "Unity of Science as a Working Hypothesis," in *Concepts, Theories, and the Mind-Body Problem,* H. Feigl, G. Maxwell and M. Scriven, eds., Minnesota Studies in the Philosophy of Science, Vol. II. Minneapolis: University of Minnesota Press, 1958.

Pitts, W. and W. S. McCulloch, "How We Know Universals," *Bulletin for Mathematical Biophysics,* Vol. IX (1947), 127-147.

Popper, K. R., "Indeterminism in Quantum Physics and Classical Physics," *British Journal for the Philosophy of Science,* Vol. I (1951), 179-188.

Putnam, Hilary, "The Analytic and the Synthetic," in *Scientific Explanation, Space, and Time,* H. Feigl and G. Maxwell, eds., Minnesota Studies in the Philosophy of Science, Vol. III. Minneapolis: University of Minnesota Press, 1962.

Quine, Willard Van Orman, "The Scope and Language of Science," *British Journal for the Philosophy of Science,* Vol. VIII (1957), 1-17.

Rashevsky, N., "Is the Concept of an Organism as a Machine a Useful One?" *Scientific Monthly,* Vol. LXXX (1955), 32-35.

Richards, P. I., "On Game-Learning Machines," *Scientific Monthly,* Vol. LXXIV (1959), 201-205.

Rogers, H., *Theory of Recursive Functions and Effective Computa-*

bility (mimeographed), Massachusetts Institute of Technology, 1957.

Rorty, Amelie O., "Slaves and Machines," *Analysis,* Vol. XXII (1962), 118-120.

Rosenbloom, Paul C., *Elements of Mathematical Logic.* New York: Dover Publications, Inc., 1951.

Ross, T., "The Synthesis of Intelligence—Its Implications," *Psychological Review,* Vol. XLV (1938), 185-189.

Rosser, B., "Extensions of Some Theorems of Gödel and Church," *Journal of Symbolic Logic,* Vol. I (1936), 87-91.

Ryle, Gilbert, *The Concept of Mind.* London: Hutchinson & Co., Ltd., 1949.

Samuel, A. L., "Some Studies in Machine Learning Using the Game of Checkers," *IBM Journal of Research and Development,* Vol. III (1959), 210-229.

Scriven, Michael, "The Compleat Robot: A Prolegomena to Androidology," in *Dimensions of Mind,* Sidney Hook, ed., pp. 118-142. New York: New York University Press, 1960.

Selfridge, O. G., "Pandemonium: A Paradigm for Learning," Massachusetts Institute of Technology, Lincoln Laboratory, Lexington, 1960.

Shannon, C. E., "A Chess-Playing Machine," *Scientific American,* Vol. CLXXXII (1950), 48-51.

———— and J. McCarthy, eds., *Automata Studies.* Princeton: Princeton University Press, 1956.

Simmons, P. L. and R. F. Simmons, *The Simulation of Cognitive Behavior, II: An Annotated Bibliography.* Santa Monica, Cal.: System Development Corporation, SP-590/002/00, 1961.

————, "The Simulation of Cognitive Processes: An Annotated Bibliography," *IRE Transactions on Electronic Computers,* EC-10, No. 3 (1961), 462-483.

Smart, J. J. C., "Gödel's Theorem, Church's Theorem and Mechanism," *Synthese,* Vol. XIII, No. 2 (1961), 105-110.

————, "Incompatible Colors," *Philosophical Studies,* Vol. X (1959), 39-42.

————, "Sensations and Brain Processes," *The Philosophical Review,* Vol. LXVIII (1959), 141-156.

Travis, L. E., "Observing how Humans Make Mistakes to Discover how to Get Computers to Do Likewise," Santa Monica, Cal.: System Development Corporation, SP-776, 1962.

Turing, A. M., "On Computable Numbers, with an Application to the Entscheidungsproblem," *Proceedings of the London Mathematical Society,* Vol. XLII (1937), 230-265.

von Neumann, John, *The Computer and the Brain.* New Haven: Yale University Press, 1958.

————, "The General and Logical Theory of Automata," *Cerebral Mechanisms in Behavior,* The Hixon Symposium, 1-31, L. A. Jefferies, ed. New York: John Wiley & Sons, Inc., 1951.

Wilkes, M. V., "Can Machines Think?" *Proceedings of the IRE,* Vol. XLI (1953), 1230-1234.

Wisdom, J. O., "The Hypothesis of Cybernetics," *British Journal for the Philosophy of Science,* Vol. II, No. 5 (1951-52), 1-24.

————, "A New Model for the Mind-Body Relationship," *British Journal for the Philosophy of Science,* Vol. II, No. 8 (1951-52), 295-301.

————, R. J. Spilsbury, and D. M. MacKay, "Symposium: Mentality in Machines," *Proceedings of the Aristotelian Society,* Supp. Vol. XXVI (1952), 1-61.

Wright, M. A., "Can Machines Be Intelligent?" *Process Control and Automation,* Vol. VI (1959), 2-6.

Ziff, Paul, *Semantic Analysis.* Ithaca: Cornell University Press, 1960.